Praying in the
WESLEYAN
SPIRIT

Praying in the
WESLEYAN SPIRIT

52 PRAYERS FOR TODAY

PAUL W. CHILCOTE

UPPER
ROOM BOOKS®
NASHVILLE

Hymns from *The Works of John Wesley*, vol. 7, *A Collection of Hymns for the Use of
the People Called Methodist*, ed. by Franz Hildebrandt and Oliver A. Beckerlegge.
Copyright © 1983 Abingdon Press. Used by permission.

Hymns from *The Unpublished Poetry of Charles Wesley*, vol. 2, *Hymns and Poems
on Holy Scripture*, ed. S T Kimbrough and Oliver A. Beckerlegge. Copyright ©
1990 Kingswood Books. Used by permission of Abingdon Press.

Cover and interior design: Bruce Gore
Typesetting: PerfecType
Cover photo: Elizabeth Etienne/Index Stock Imagery
Background text on cover: Original letter by John Wesley from the collection of
    The Upper Room® Museum, Nashville, Tennessee
First Printing: 2001

            Library of Congress Cataloging-in-Publication Data
Chilcote, Paul Wesley, 1954–
    Praying in the Wesleyan spirit: 52 prayers for today/by Paul Wesley
        Chilcote.
        p. cm.
    Includes indexes.
    ISBN 0-8358-0950-1
        1. Methodist Church—Prayer-books and devotions—English. 2. Wesley,
    John, 1703–1791. 3. Wesley, Charles, 1707–1788. I. Wesley, John,
    1703–1791. II. Wesley, Charles, 1707–1788. III. Title.

BX8337 .C48 2001
242'.807—dc21   2001017373

In memory of my mother,
LOUISE CHILCOTE,
my first teacher in prayer

Contents

Preface

I HAVE ALWAYS believed that if people read John Wesley's sermons, many lives would be changed. His sermons bear witness to a vision of the Christian life that is oriented around the simple message of "faith working by love." Certainly this word needs to be spoken and heard in our own day. But for many people Wesley's sermons are inaccessible. They were written by a priest of the Church of England in the eighteenth century. The language is archaic to our ears. The structure is linear, logical, and somewhat wooden. While described as sermons, they are really theological essays, meant not so much to be preached or heard as to be read and reflected upon. They contain many important truths concerning the Christian faith, but the packaging is off-putting to many.

In a little book entitled *Wesley Speaks on Christian Vocation* I made an effort to modernize and abridge a number of the more important sermons and treatises of the Wesleys. Others have done the same thing, most notably Tom Oden in his "modern English edition" of five Wesley sermons entitled *The New Birth*. But all of these efforts have been only samplings. The Fifty-three Sermons of John Wesley, forty-four of which are considered to be doctrinal standards by most branches of the Wesleyan tradition, are a veritable mine of spiritual insight and wisdom. They need to be reclaimed today in a form that is both faithful and accessible.

At the same time I was pondering how to present these sermons in a way that would be spiritually uplifting for the modern reader, my interest in St. Benedict led me to a little volume on his Rule by John McQuiston II. In *Always We Begin Again: The Benedictine Way of Living,* the author essentially "translated," or paraphrased, Benedict's work into his own words. Not so much concerned with producing a precisely accurate statement of the original, McQuiston wanted to make the Rule of St. Benedict available to the lay reader of theology, to capture the spirit of the original in an engaging contemporary form. I have attempted to create here the same accessibility to the sermons of John Wesley.

In this collection of fifty-two sermons (I have omitted his funeral sermon on the life of George Whitefield) I have gone one step further. Not only is each sermon modernized and encapsulated in a brief page or two; the content of the sermons is transformed into prayers that are personal and can be used devotionally. Nothing could be more consistent with the original purpose of the sermons, for the Wesleyan way has always been a way of devotion. It is also a way rooted in the scriptures. And since Wesley provided the scripture texts for these sermons, I have also included them for your study and reflection. So your journey through these prayers will carry you through the fertile soil of God's Word as well. While not being slavish to Wesley's language, I have tried to stay as close to the original titles of the sermons in the headings for each reading. Wesley published thirteen sermons on Jesus' Sermon on the Mount in this collection, and instead of simply numbering them, as he did, I have given them separate, descriptive titles.

In addition to the biblical texts and the prayers, you will find relevant excerpts from the amazing hymns of Charles Wesley for each selection. One of the great saints of the early church said that to sing is to pray twice. Here is an opportunity, therefore, to expand your experience of prayer. Again nothing could be more Wesleyan. In fact, most of the early Methodist people "learned their theology" by singing it. The Methodist movement, under the direction of the Wesley brothers, was born in song. Each of these selections from Charles' lyrical theology is tied to the text and theme of the sermon it accompanies. Most of them will be new to even the most devoted Methodist, and that is intentional. But there are also some hymns that are familiar enough to elicit wonderful memories of singing our faith.

While I have been very intentional in my use of inclusive language with regard to the prayers, the hymns of Charles Wesley present a peculiar challenge. I considered the possibility of revising the hymns in order to make then inclusive as well, but this raised concerns about their poetic integrity. After consulting with colleagues, I decided to retain the original, historic forms. It is my sincere hope that the masculine language does not create an artificial barrier to anyone who seeks to meet the God who gave us our birth and loves us all. That is the inclusive God of whom Charles Wesley sang. Most importantly, I hope these hymn texts will enable the Spirit to touch your life in a different way than the prayers themselves do.

For Methodists of virtually every stripe, both head and heart are important. If head and heart are working together as they should, then hands inevitably get involved as well! What better way for people to encounter this rich treasury of Christian witness than to pray it and sing it, and then to put it into action. If this is your first encounter with these formative sermons and hymns of the Wesleyan tradition, my prayer is that you will be transformed as you pray them. If I have failed in any way to be faithful to the spirit of my own mentors in the Christian faith, John and Charles Wesley, my hope is that God will find some way to engage your heart, head, and hands so as to birth your faith anew or nurture it to still greater depths. The Wesleyan way of living the Christian faith is dynamic and profoundly relational. It is a process of faith working by love leading to holiness of heart and life. Walk with Christ through these prayers, both read and sung, and invite the Holy Spirit to be your companion along the way. God be with you on the journey.

ALL SAINTS' DAY, 2000
Paul Wesley Chilcote

Introduction

JOHN WESLEY (1703–91) was one of the greatest preachers of all time. In a lifetime that spanned nearly a century, he preached no fewer than forty thousand sermons. His preaching became one of the hallmarks of the revival he spearheaded within the Church of England. His methods of reform were distinctive, and they were also controversial in his day. Instead of waiting for people to come to him to hear his message of God's grace and love, he took the good news of Jesus Christ to them wherever they were. He began his so-called "field preaching" in 1739, and it is probably right to date the beginning of the evangelical revival and the birth of Methodism from the events of that year.

During the previous year, however, in 1738, both John and his brother Charles (1707–88) experienced God's presence in their lives in a profoundly transforming way. While both were priests in the Church of England with many years of ministry between them (even a period as missionaries to the infant colony of Georgia), the dynamic, relational quality of living faith was lacking in their lives. Perhaps it is right to say that they knew a lot about God, but they had never really "met" God in the person of Jesus Christ. They knew that love was at the center—the heart—of God. They had committed the entirety of their lives to the church they loved. They were the servants (if not yet the true brothers) of Christ. But they had never felt the unconditional love of God.

Like many Christians, even Christians today, the Wesley brothers believed that they first had to make themselves acceptable to God. I don't believe any two seekers after God could have worked harder. But in 1738, both of them, just several days apart, made one of the most important discoveries of their lives. They realized that God had loved them all along. Like a spiritual sunrise, it dawned on them that God's presence and love had accompanied them each step of their journey. Like St. Paul they knew they needed to do nothing to win God's love; rather God's love was always there, freely offered to them in Jesus Christ. They experienced the deepest meaning of God's grace. The unconditional love of God in Christ freed them and opened up to them a whole new world of joy, peace, and inner healing.

Most of John Wesley's sermons were about this important discovery and its ripple effects in the life of the believer. What John Wesley preached, his brother Charles put into hymns—thousands of hymns. The Methodist movement then was formed upon this shared experience of salvation by grace—a faith that had to be sung. The more John preached and Charles sang the gospel through his verse, the more people were spiritually liberated. The Spirit of God was alive and at work in the hearts and minds of many people, especially poor people, who had never known God as Someone real in their lives before.

Small groups or communities called Societies formed around this common experience of God's grace and love. The Wesleys and other kindred spirits provided the leadership and guidance needed to establish a firm foundation for this growing movement. Together they prayed, studied God's Word, helped each other grow in their newfound faith, and celebrated their family meal—the

Lord's Supper. All these activities strengthened their faith and empowered them to be Christ's faithful disciples in ministry to God's world. Indeed, they all viewed mission—the proclamation of God's love in word and deed, in witness and service—as the reason for their existence. The Methodist Societies gathered together to learn how to love and were then sent out to share that love with others, singing their faith along the way.

In order for others to better understand this growing movement in the life of the church and to explain more fully to his followers exactly what they believed, John Wesley began to publish his sermons. These carefully selected sermons functioned both to defend Methodism (as an "apology" or defense) and to teach the Methodist people (as a "catechism" or manual of instruction). Since Wesley never viewed his movement as a departure from his beloved Church of England, either in what he believed or what he practiced, it was important for others to know this clearly. He published four volumes of sermons between 1746 and 1760. In later years, as the ranks of Wesley's itinerant preachers began to swell, he determined that the forty-four sermons contained in these volumes would function as a distinctive "doctrinal standard" for the Methodist people. If anyone felt called to preach in Wesley's "Connexion"—his renewal movement within the church—he or she was required to know and accept these teachings.

Nine sermons were later added to the original forty-four in order to clarify some points and to address new issues. While these additional sermons (eight of which are included here) were never given the same authoritative status as the original collection, they were important to the early Methodists. John wrote all of these sermons except Sermon III, "Awake, Thou That Sleepest," which his brother Charles had preached at Oxford University. The essential content of all these sermons is re-presented in this volume in the form of prayers.

It might seem strange, but John Wesley did not preach all of the sermons he published. In fact, the sermons reflected here were intended more for reading in the context of private study than for hearing in a setting of public worship. They are more like "sermonic essays," intended to instruct and inform, not to entertain.

Wesley's preaching, in general, was very different in form, if not in substance, from these written essays. For one thing, he very seldom preached from a prepared manuscript. He spoke extemporaneously and from the "heart." This is not to say that he abandoned the "head" or encouraged others to nurture an "unthinking faith." Rather both Wesley brothers believed that when head and heart are held together, then our hands get involved as well. Eyewitnesses to their public preaching frequently comment about its urgency, practicality, and relevance for real life. "Now is the day of salvation" was John Wesley's implicit, if not explicit, text for virtually every sermon he preached. Every sermon, in one way or another, called for a gracious response to God's grace, lived out in a real world.

Wesley's published sermons, likewise, are both theological and practical. Rather than being dry, academic studies in theology, they are intended to teach about and touch real life. In one of the prefaces to his sermons, in fact, Wesley says that he has intentionally used "plain words for plain people." These sermons are for everyone. Their primary purpose, as was the case for all of Wesley's "theology," is transformational. The sermons are concerned with practical matters of the faith. They revolve around issues related to personal and social salvation and how the Christian is called to live out her or his faith daily. So rather than coming across as cold and detached, the sermons have a certain warmth about them. They seem to be answering the questions of common, ordinary people—questions about how our life with God is restored, how our broken lives are healed, and how we are to become more loving—rather than answering questions that no one seems to be asking.

The sermons are variations on the theme of the Wesleys' distinctive understanding of salvation. They emphasize the centrality of grace, the view of faith as pardon and reconciliation, and the assurance of God's mercy confirmed by the Spirit of Christ. They describe how God works in our lives to make us whole. The healing and restoration of happiness and holiness to our lives is a pervasive theme. The "law of love," revealed to us by Christ, defines the essence of what it means to be a Christian. It is noteworthy that no fewer than thirteen of these sermons are Wesley's reflections upon Jesus' Sermon on the Mount. The sermons are all about God's grace and the fullness of God's grace in our lives.

Another interesting thing to note in these sermons is how Wesley holds together aspects of the Christian faith that often are torn apart. Faith and works are presented as distinct but not separate. Likewise, personal and social dimensions of life in Christ, the form and the power of godliness, Word and Sacrament, truth and unity, faith and love are all held together. This distinctive, consistent pattern reflects the central theme of Wesley's own life and ministry, namely, that of "faith working by love leading to holiness of heart and life." The Wesleys not only proclaimed this message boldly in their preaching, they lived it. They practiced what they preached.

What may be of even greater significance is the fact that the Wesleys practiced what they sang. Some scholars have gone so far as to argue that without the hymns of Charles Wesley there never would have been a Wesleyan revival. Of all the collections of hymns that the two brothers published over the course of the eighteenth century, no hymnbook was of greater importance than the 1780 *A Collection of Hymns for the Use of the People called Methodists* (from which most of the selections here are drawn). These hymns functioned as a primer of theology for the Methodist people, reflecting the same concerns and themes that dominate the Wesleys' preaching. But they also served as a devotional manual for praying in the Wesleyan spirit. The faith of a Methodist, it must always be remembered, is a faith that sings.

A final, more personal word. My first introduction to the sermons of John Wesley was through the eyes of his contemporaries, particularly women. I was fascinated by their accounts of his ministry in their diaries, journals, and letters. Wesley's preaching was always central in these personal reflections. The "nowness"—the urgency—of Wesley's message and his preaching is immediately evident in these accounts. He was concerned about the brokenness of people's lives and the power of God in Christ to make them whole. He simply offered Christ to all as best he could, got out of the way, and watched God's Spirit work. He was constantly amazed by the power of unconditional love. This message resounds in all the sermons.

Later I worked my way through the "standard sermons" in

a deliberate and systematic way. I am convinced that these sermons are an important legacy, not only for the people called Methodist but for the larger Christian community as well. They are a rich treasury of spiritual insight. meant both to change and to guide lives. They open up for us innumerable windows to the multiple dimensions of God's love. That is why Wesley published them. He wanted the people of his own day to experience God's love, to be transformed by it, and to grow into the most loving people they could be in this life. My hope is that the prayer form of his sermons you encounter here will have that same effect.

Suggestions for Using These Readings

~

THERE ARE A number of ways that you can use this resource. Perhaps the most obvious way is to center each week of the year on one of the readings. You may read the selection on Sunday, at the beginning of the week, or read it daily throughout the course of the week. In this way you will immerse yourself in the Wesleyan way through the course of a full year. You may actually want to obtain a copy of Wesley's sermons and read them in their entirety in conjunction with these prayers.

Another possibility is to use the prayers at the beginning and ending of each day. If you were to pray selections one and two on the first day, three and four on the second, and so forth through fifty-two, you would be able to make your way through the entire collection in the course of a month (actually twenty-six days with Sundays left out for other religious practices and corporate worship). The liturgical seasons of Advent and Lent would be particularly appropriate times for this approach.

Yet another option is to read the prayers in their entirety, straight through. This approach gives you the big picture. To have a sense of the whole is often helpful. Since these are prayers, they do call for a more devotional pace of reading. Time for reflection— allowing the prayers to sink into your spirit—is also important. A day apart might provide the opportunity to read through the prayers in a more leisurely and spiritually uplifting way.

In a separate appendix I have provided a listing of the scriptural texts associated with each prayer/sermon in their canonical order. You may prefer to read through these selections in the order of the texts, giving attention to and time for meditation upon each of the passages. Note the amazing range and diversity of texts that John Wesley used. There is great breadth and depth here.

These selections might be put to use in corporate contexts, for example, in prayer groups, covenant discipleship groups, Bible studies, class meetings, and Sunday or midweek worship. The prayers can be read in unison, used responsively, or coordinated with worship themes and sermons. You may have occasion to study the Sermon on the Mount, for instance, and find the thirteen prayers related to these texts particularly fruitful as discussion starters or acts of devotion.

Open yourself to the leading of the Spirit. However you choose to use this book, approach the experience prayerfully. Ask God to speak to you through the insights of the Wesleys and their vision of the Christian way. Once you have engaged in prayer using these texts, think about what steps you need to take to put their message into action, to live them out in your daily life. In this faith working by love we experience God's transforming power in our lives.

All of Wesley's sermons are collected in the first four volumes of The Works of John Wesley, edited by Albert Outler and published by Abingdon Press. This is a definitive scholarly edition. A more accessible one-volume collection is *John Wesley's Sermons: An Anthology,* edited by Albert Outler and Richard Heitzenrater, also published by Abingdon.

1 ☙
Salvation by Faith

Scripture:

> For by grace you have been saved through faith.
>
> —*Ephesians 2:8*

Prayer:

Gracious God,

All the blessings I have experienced in my life are gifts from
you.

I know I have done nothing to deserve them.

And the greatest blessing of all, salvation, I receive from you
as a gift by grace through faith in Jesus Christ.

Help me to move beyond simply knowing about you
into a vital relationship with you based on trust,
into a life rooted in Jesus Christ that brings peace and
power, as I rely on his death and resurrection in my
daily living.

You offer to me a present salvation,
a liberation from the guilt and fear and power of sin.

Birth within me a burning desire to flee from all habitual and
willful sin.

Cleanse my heart and make me clean.

When I am tempted to think that faith is all I need,

remind me that the purpose of faith is the restoration of
   true holiness in my heart and life.
Faith is always a means to love's end.
   May I never rest in my faith as if it were an end in itself;
      rather help me to rely on your love as I seek to live
      faithfully.
   May all the good that I am able to accomplish in your
      strength lead me away from pride or boasting
      and always point to you as the source of all that is good.
I know that I am safe and held in your arms whenever I
   put my entire trust in you. Give me courage to
   proclaim this wonderful news to all those around me
   who long to find their way home, and when I proclaim
   faith in Christ, and others turn away, may I ever rest in
   the victory of your love. Amen.

Hymn:

   Infinite, unexhausted Love!
      Jesus and love are one:
   If still to me thy mercies move
      They are restrained to none.

   What shall I do my God to love,
      My loving God to praise?
   The length, and breadth, and height to prove,
      And depth of sovereign grace?

   Thy sovereign grace to all extends,
      Immense and unconfined:
   From age to age it never ends;
      It reaches all mankind.

(Collection 207:1, 2, 3)

2 ❧
Altogether Christian

Scripture:

> Are you so quickly persuading me to become a Christian?
>
> —*Acts 26:28*

Prayer:

O Life-giving Creator,
  Sometimes I feel like "almost a Christian."
    I am committed to justice;
    I try to be honest and loving;
    You could say, in a sense, that I have the form of godliness,
      but I lack the power of your love in my life.
  I obey your laws:
    I am patient and kind to others;
    I help my neighbor as much as I can;
    I pray, read your Word, enjoy the sacrament of Holy
      Communion, and set apart sacred time to be with you.
    I am absolutely sincere when I say
      I want you to be in the center of my life
      and want to serve you from the bottom of my heart.
  But despite all my efforts, I still feel like I am "almost a
    Christian."
  Make me "altogether a Christian," O recreating God.

Fill my heart to overflowing with your love.
Enable me to love my neighbor as I love myself.
Plant within me a sure trust and confidence that
    Christ died for me and loves me still.
Let love be the test of my faith, O God.
Help me to be *altogether* and not simply *almost* a Christian.
Amen.

Hymn:

Master, I own thy lawful claim;
    Thine, wholly thine, I long to be!
Thou seest at last I willing am
    Where'er thou goest to follow thee,
Myself in all things to deny,
Thine, wholly thine, to live and die.

Wherefore to thee I all resign;
    Being thou art, and love, and power;
Thy only will be done, not mine!
    Thee, Lord, let earth and heaven adore!
Flow back the rivers to the sea,
And let our all be lost in thee!

(Collection 323:1, 5)

3 ☙
Spiritual Awakenings

Scripture:

> Sleeper, awake! Rise from the dead, and Christ will
> shine on you.

> *—Ephesians 5:14*

Prayer:

Renewing and Refreshing God,
  How desperately your children need to be awakened from
    their sleep!
  As I look around me in my world, so many people live in
    darkness:
    They have no concern for their need of you, are satisfied in
      their sins, content in their brokenness, and arrogant in
      their self-centered complacency.
    But they are not really alive, God, not as you want them
      to be.
    They are really dead and blind, with no power to be who
      you have created them to be, no senses to discern your
      dream and vision for their lives. They seem to be in a
      deep, deep sleep.
  Wake them up, God. Help them to see what is real and what
    is illusion.

Help them to see who they are and to whom they really
belong.
Help them to reclaim their true identity as your children,
as creatures who have your image woven into their
humanity,
who are partakers of your own divine nature,
who can be changed inwardly, born again, and renewed
by the power of the Holy Spirit in their lives.
May they hear your still small voice within, O Lord, and
awaken in faith to the promises that are theirs in Christ.
To all who awake and arise, you promise the Light.
You promise to dwell—to set up your home—
in our hearts.
You promise liberation from sin through the gift of
your Holy Spirit
who comes into our lives, filling us with love.
You promise not only the form of godliness but the
power that makes us truly righteous, winsome,
loving, and pure.
Awaken us all by the truth and simplicity of your good news
which is proclaimed in your promises to every human
being,
that we might feel the spirit of Christ in us and
among us,
singing in our heart that we are the children of God.
Amen.

Hymn:

> Speak with that voice which wakes the dead
>> And bid the sleeper rise;
> And bid his guilty conscience dread
>> The death that never dies.
>
> I must this instant now begin
>> Out of my sleep to wake,
> And turn to God, and every sin
>> Continually forsake.

(Collection 81:5, 7)

4 🐦
Scriptural Christianity

Scripture:

> And they were all filled with the Holy Spirit.
>
> —*Acts 4:31*

Prayer:

Wonderful God of Word and Promise,
> To be filled with your Spirit is such an inexpressible gift;
>> to have the mind that was in Christ and to bear the fruits
>> of the Spirit is what being a Christian is all about.

It is your Spirit that enables me to cry out, "Abba, Father,"
> your Spirit bearing witness with my spirit that I am your
> child.

The very essence of my faith is a sure trust and confidence in
your love,
> and because of that confidence, my soul, like Mary's,
> glorifies you, and my spirit rejoices in you.

Since your love wells up within me and continues to grow
daily, how could I do anything other than love my
brothers and sisters
> who surround me with their joys and their needs?

Lord, I want to be humble, gentle, patient, and generous;
> save me from passion and pride, lust and vanity, ambition
> and envy.

Feed me from the twin tables of your Word and sacrament
and meet me there as you have promised,
so that I might refrain from evil
and have a deep longing in my spirit always to do good.
Lord, I pray that my faith in and love for you is both visible
and contagious.
I want my light to shine for you;
I want people to see your love in me in such a way that
they will turn to you again;
I want to be a witness to your love even when my
motivations are misunderstood by those I seek to love
for your sake.
I long for the time when all people will know you
and claim their place in your family.
What a glorious world that would be,
filled with peace, reconciliation, and justice;
everyone looking out for the other;
all malice, envy, and revenge removed;
no unkind words, no deception or bitterness.
All things would reflect your reign, and hearts would be
filled with love.
O God who has revealed yourself to us in your Word,
this is true, scriptural Christianity, but where does it now
exist?
Are those who have authority filled with the Holy Spirit?
Are those who teach bearing the fruits of indwelling love?
Are those who lead in the church patterns to the rest?
Have the young in faith been offered a vision of their high
calling and the adventure of life in you?
Give us the gifts of integrity and authenticity in our
relationships with you, with one another,
and with ourselves,

and help us to be truly loving people.
We know that only you can plant
the seed of your love in our lives. Amen.

Hymn:

Happy the souls that first believed,
To Jesus and each other cleaved,
Joined by the unction from above
In mystic fellowship of love.

With grace abundantly endued,
A pure, believing multitude,
They all were of one heart and soul,
And only love inspired the whole.

(Collection 16:1, 3)

5 🐟
Justification by Faith

Scripture:

> But to one who without works trusts him who justifies
> the ungodly, such faith is reckoned as righteousness.
>
> —*Romans 4:5*

Prayer:

O Righteous and Pardoning God,
  How can we make our way back to you and find your love
    when we are so broken and sinful?
We were made in your own image, holy and perfect in love,
    with your righteousness woven into the very fabric of our
      being.
But we rebelled against you, O God, and died inwardly
    because our disobedience and pride separated us
      from you.
Your love for us was too strong to leave us cut off and
    alienated,
      and so you sent us your Son to offer us your
        forgiveness,
        to invite us home and restore our relationship
          with you.
What love is this—my soul soars simply to think of it—

that reaches out to each of us and freely offers us
restoration and life to each of us through your beloved
Son, Jesus Christ?
We ponder what it means to be reconciled to you and live
with you again:
It does not mean that we are yet holy through and
through.
It does not mean that we are freed from sin entirely.
It does not mean that we deceive you, claiming for
ourselves more than we are.
But it does mean, O Blessed God, that you have pardoned
us and forgiven us of all our sins!
And to whom do you offer this precious gift,
O Gracious God?
It is the ungodly and the sinner that you call your own.
It is the lost sheep that the Good Shepherd seeks so
earnestly in the darkness of the night.
It is those of us who already stand condemned
—at death's door as it were—whom you seek with
all your heart.
We know that there is nothing we could ever do to deserve
your love,
and yet you choose to offer it still, like a loving parent
whose love can never die.
And how do we receive this precious gift, O Generous God?
You gift us with faith that it might be our own.
You plant in the depths of our souls a sure trust and
confidence that you have forgiven and will forgive us
through Christ.
The only thing we need to find our way back to your loving
embrace is faith. No other conditions stand in our way.
You provide for us exactly what we need.

Having accepted your wondrous gift,
   the gift of your unconditional love in Jesus Christ,
      we experience pardon;
      we know what it means truly to be free. Amen.

Hymn:

   Jesu, thy blood and righteousness
   My beauty are, my glorious dress;
   'Midst flaming worlds, in these arrayed,
   With joy shall I lift up my head.

   Jesu, be endless praise to thee,
   Whose boundless mercy hath for me—
   For me, and all thy hands have made—
   An everlasting ransom paid.

(Collection 183:1, 8)

6 ✍

The Righteousness of Faith

Scripture:

> Moses writes concerning the righteousness that comes
> from the law, that "the person who does these things will
> live by them." But the righteousness that comes from
> faith says, "Do not say in your heart, 'Who will ascend
> into heaven?'" (that is, to bring Christ down) "or 'Who
> will descend into the abyss?'" (that is, to bring Christ up
> from the dead). But what does it say? "The word is near
> you, on your lips and in your heart" (that is, the word of
> faith that we proclaim).
>
> —*Romans 10:5-8*

Prayer:

O God of Grace and Truth,
> How foolish it is for me to attempt to build a relationship
> > with you on the basis of my own effort
> > and goodness!
> What a difference there is between a life founded upon your grace
> > and a life based in the law!
> If being reconciled to you required a life based upon the law,
> > then I would have to be perfectly obedient to the law,
> > > without exception from beginning to end.

The righteousness of faith, however, requires only trust in the
new covenant that you have established in Jesus Christ.
Strictly speaking, this covenant of grace does not
require me to *do* anything, only to *believe*.
Graciously you say to me, "Believe in the Lord Jesus Christ,
and you shall be saved and live."
My childlike trust in Jesus Christ frees me from the guilt of
my sin and empowers me to serve others in his love.
What a difference there is between the covenant of works
and of grace:
the first assumes that I am already holy and happy;
the second, that I have fallen short of God's
loving image;
the first requires perfect obedience to every point of
the law;
the second requires only faith;
the first demands that I pay the price for my sin myself;
the second demands only that I believe in him who
paid the price for me;
the first calls for me to do something beyond my ability;
the second calls for me to acknowledge something
very close at hand—to say in my heart—
God is love!
How foolish it is to trust in the righteousness of the law;
how wise to submit to that righteousness rooted in my
trust of you.
For if I put my trust in my own goodness, I set out in the
wrong direction—my first step is a fundamental
mistake.
But if I put my trust in Christ, then my entire life is
founded upon your

liberating grace, your free love, and your undeserved
mercy.
Here is true wisdom—here is true happiness—to rest
faithfully in the righteousness of faith.
Help me to understand, gracious Lord, that true forgiveness
and communion with you is not based upon doing the
right things or becoming good enough to win
your love.
You do not say, "Do this"; rather you say, "Believe in the Lord
Jesus Christ,
and you shall be saved." Amen.

Hymn:

Oft I in my heart have said,
    Who shall ascend on high?
Mount to Christ my glorious head,
    And bring him from the sky?
Borne on contemplation's wing,
    Surely I should find him there,
Where the angels praise their King,
    And gain the morning star.

But the righteousness of faith
    Hath taught me better things:
'Inward turn thine eyes' (it saith,
    While Christ to me it brings),
'Christ is ready to impart
    Life to all for life who sigh;
In thy mouth, and in thy heart,
    The word is ever nigh.'

(Collection 185:1, 3)

7 ✌
The Way to Shalom

Scripture:

> The kingdom of God has come near; repent, and believe
> in the good news.
>
> —*Mark 1:15*

Prayer:

Sovereign God,
In Christ you have shown us that to be truly religious means
to live in your reign—to live in and for shalom.
True religion does not have to do with what we eat or drink,
with observing religious rituals, forms, and ceremonies,
with believing the right things,
or with performing good works (although true religion
naturally leads to them from the heart).
True religion consists of righteousness, peace, and joy in the
Holy Spirit.
True religion means loving you with our whole being
and loving our neighbors as ourselves.
Such a love—which we receive from you as a gift—fulfills
all laws and is the totality of what it means
to be a Christian.
Lord, you long to fill our lives with happiness

as well as holiness.
You want to give us a peace that passes all understanding
and a joy that is possible only with hearts rooted in
your love.
All of this is nothing other than shalom—
wholeness and happiness,
justice, peace, and joy—present and potent wherever Jesus
is preached.
Through the good news of Jesus Christ, you have shown us,
O God,
how to find our way into your reign of peace:
The first step is *repentance;*
everything begins in true self-knowledge,
in the acknowledgment of our brokenness,
our lack of trust in you and your will to save us,
our impotence to rise above our sin,
our pride and self-centered blindness.
Simply acknowledging our helplessness and
our need for you
puts us close to your reign in our lives.
But the next and most important step is *trust;*
everything comes to its fruition in our believing your
good news.
So help us to move in our lives, O liberating Love,
from belief in the truth of the Bible and the creeds,
from our knowledge about you and your ways,
to a sure trust and confidence in your
pardoning mercy!
Through the life, death, and resurrection of Jesus
you have revealed
your whole vision of what life is meant to be,
and if we root our lives in that vision,

united with Christ,
then we find peace and joy, and your love fills
our hearts. Amen.

Hymn:

O that I could repent,
O that I could believe!
Thou, by thy voice, the marble rent,
    The rock in sunder cleave!
    Thou by thy two-edged sword
    My soul and spirit part;
Strike, with the hammer of thy word,
    And break my stubborn heart!

Saviour, and Prince of peace,
    The double grace bestow,
Unloose the bands of wickedness,
    And let the captive go;
    Grant me my sins to feel,
    And then the load remove;
Wound, and pour in, my wounds to heal,
    The balm of pard'ning love.

(Collection 102:1, 2)

8 🖎
No Condemnation

Scripture:

> There is therefore now no condemnation for those who
> are in Christ Jesus . . . , who walk not according to the
> flesh but according to the Spirit.
>
> —*Romans 8:1-4*

Prayer:

Forgiving God,
   One of your greatest gifts to those who believe in Christ Jesus
      is freedom from condemnation, either your own—
         having been reconciled through Christ,
      or our own—having rediscovered our true identity as
         your children.
   What a joy it is to live our life in Christ:
      to believe in his name and to be united to him,
      to pursue virtue, rather than being destroyed by lust,
      to strive for the most lofty and noble ideals,
      to dream your dreams and embrace your vision for
         our life,
         and to manifest the fruits of the Spirit—like patience,
         kindness, and gentleness—in our life.

What a blessing it is, Lord, to know that you do not
    condemn us
    for our past or present sins,
    for inward sin, even as we continue to struggle against it,
    for sins that arise from our physical and emotional
        brokenness,
    and even for sins that take us by surprise.
        Despite the fact that we are frequently grieved
            by what we say and do
                and feel guilty because of our failure,
            we are able to pick ourselves up
                and move on toward your loving purpose
                    because in Christ we are no longer condemned.
Since you have forgiven us in Christ, we do not have to fear
    any longer!
You empower us to overcome the destructive patterns and
    behaviors that remain but no longer have a grip
    on our lives.
Although we are still weak in many ways,
    you affirm us,
        strengthen our faith,
            and lead us home! Amen.

Hymn:

        Long my imprisoned spirit lay,
            Fast bound in sin and nature's night.
        Thine eye diffused a quick'ning ray;
            I woke; the dungeon flamed with light.
        My chains fell off, my heart was free,
        I rose, went forth, and followed thee.

No condemnation now I dread,
  Jesus, and all in him, is mine.
Alive in him, my living head,
  And clothed in righteousness divine,
Bold I approach th'eternal throne,
And claim the crown, through Christ my own.

(Collection 193:4, 5)

9 🦢
From Fear to Love

Scripture:

> For you did not receive a spirit of slavery to fall back into fear, but you have received a spirit of adoption. [And so] we cry, "Abba! Father!"
>
> —*Romans 8:15*

Prayer:

Loving Parent God,

When I look at the children you have created to be a part of your family,

I see three kinds of people:

those who neither fear nor love you (they seem to be the vast majority of the human race);

those who fear you, but their fear is a terrible burden;

those who have recovered their true identity in Christ— who have exchanged their fear for love.

How tragic it is to witness the lives of those who simply sleep through life.

They truly believe that they are free, but they are in the bondage of ignorance and unfettered selfishness.

They do not know you or care to know you, and they do not know themselves.

But those who have come to know you and themselves in
    relation to you may be in bondage still.
    For those convicted of their sin realize how far
        they are from what you call them to be.
        For them the pleasing dream, delusive rest, false peace,
           and vain security of the sleeper is vanished.
    Instead, they are filled with fear by a sense of your
    righteousness.
    Realizing how impotent they are, eventually they
        cry out to you,
        "Who shall deliver me?"
All praise to you, merciful God, for those who discover
    their true identity in you
    exchange their fear for grace and love.
Their eyes are open to see the loving, gracious God. They
    experience your pardoning love in their lives through
    their faith in Jesus Christ.
    They are released from the guilt and power of sin;
    they no longer fear your wrath;
    they have freedom from sin;
    they not only strive against but have victory over sin.
In short, they have received the spirit of adoption. Having
    once been outside your loving embrace, they now feel the
    arms of your love around them.
May all of your children come to know what it means to live
    in your grace,
    to be members of your family by adoption.
    Grant to every child the joyous light of heaven
        here on earth,
        the gift of true inner peace,
        the liberty of living as your child,

and victory over all those forces that separate us from
  your unconditional love.
Help us all to strive for the high mark of our calling
  in Christ. Help us to move from sleep through fear
  and into the depth of your love for us all. Amen.

Hymn:

Since the Son hath made me free,
Let me taste my liberty;
Thee behold with open face,
Triumph in thy saving grace,
Thy great will delight to prove,
Glory in thy perfect love.

Abba, Father! hear thy child,
Late in Jesus reconciled;
Hear, and all the graces shower,
All the joy, and peace, and power,
All my Saviour asks above,
All the life and heaven of love.

(Collection 379:1, 2)

10 🖎
The Witness of the Spirit

Scripture:

> It is that very Spirit bearing witness with our spirit that we
> are children of God.
>
> —*Romans 8:16*

Prayer:

Spirit of the Living God,
    It is so easy to fall into religious fanaticism—
        mistaking my own imagination for your voice
          on the one hand
        or denying the possibility of a close personal relationship
          with you—closing my ears to the still small voice
          within—on the other.
    And yet how important it is for your Spirit to bear witness to
        my spirit that I belong to you and that I am loved.
    There are times, O God, when I genuinely feel that
        I am your child.
        My own spirit exults in the fact that you have called me
          by my name.
        I love you and I love my neighbor because the Spirit
          whispers, deep down inside, that you have
          loved me first.

I have no doubts about who I am and to whom I belong,
in spite of the fact that your love for me still remains a
great mystery.
But how do I know that all of this is not just wishful thinking?
How do I know that this is not just some kind of
self-deception?
It seems to me that your Holy Word is very clear about
what must precede, accompany, and follow this
wonderful feeling of wholeness and well-being that
comes from you.
Repentance—truly knowing my inmost self—will always
precede my experience of your pardoning
love and acceptance.
Humble joy will fill my heart if the Spirit is truly with me.
And if I truly love you, I certainly will follow your
commandments and always seek to do your will.
Lord, if I am not lowly of heart, not gentle or meek, not
obedient to your law of love, then I am simply deceiving
myself. I have not yet learned what it means to be your
child. In those moments, forgive me.
The genuine influence of your Spirit upon my heart will be
known by the fruits of that same Spirit. That is the most
critical test. Thanks be to you, Heart of my own heart, for
the gift of knowing I belong to you and that I can bear fruit
that others might taste and see how wonderful is your love.
Amen.

Hymn:

> We by his Spirit prove
> And know the things of God;
> The things which freely of his love

He hath on us bestowed:
His Spirit to us he gave,
And dwells in us, we know;
The witness in ourselves we have,
And all his fruits we show.

The meek and lowly heart,
That in our Saviour was,
To us his Spirit does impart,
And signs us with his cross:
Our nature's turned, our mind
Transformed in all its powers;
And both the witnesses are joined,
The Spirit of God with ours.

(Collection 93:4, 5)

11 ❧
Assurance and Its Fruit

Scripture:

> It is that very Spirit bearing witness with our spirit that we
> are children of God.

—*Romans 8:16*

Prayer:

O Intimate God,

We need the assurance that we are your children, an inner
voice reminding us we belong to you. In our journey with
Christ, we want to avoid both formalism, which lacks
intimacy, and fanaticism, which can lead to spiritual pride.
We want Christ's spirit in our hearts.

Grant us, therefore, gracious Lord, an immediate and direct
testimony of your Holy Spirit that we are your children,
that Christ loves us all and gave himself for us in order to
heal our broken lives and restore our fellowship with you.
When stormy winds and troubled seas begin to
overwhelm us,
calm our hearts as they rest in the arms of Jesus.

Since we cannot love you fully until we know that
you love us,
send us your Spirit, so that heaven

might spring up in our hearts.
Not only must our consciences be clear,
    not only must we be sincere,
we need to know that you claim us as your own
    and adopt us into your family of love.
This witness in our hearts is not meant to prove anything;
    rather its purpose is to assure us of your love.
    The genuine witness will be known by the fruit it produces
        in our lives.
    When you assure us of your love, our lives are changed,
        both on the inside and the outside.
        We may experience severe trials in life, but we also find
            your grace in the midst of them.
        And in all things, you give us meek and lowly hearts,
            for your love can never express itself through us in a
            proud and uncharitable way.
The assurance that we are your children, loving God, precedes
    its fruit in our lives. We love because you first loved us.
    May the witness of your Spirit in our lives be fruitful in
        every way, and may the spiritual fruit of our lives be
        rooted firmly in your love, mercy, and grace. Amen.

Hymn:

I want the spirit of power within,
    Of love, and of a healthful mind:
Of power to conquer inbred sin,
    Of love to thee and all mankind,
Of health, that pain and death defies,
Most vig'rous when the body dies.

O that the Comforter would come!
Nor visit as a transient guest,
But fix in me his constant home,
And take possession of my breast;
And fix in me his loved abode,
The temple of indwelling God!

(Collection 365:1, 3)

12 ❧
Christian Conscience

Scripture:

> Indeed, this is our boast, the testimony of our conscience:
> we have behaved in the world with frankness and godly
> sincerity, not by earthly wisdom but by the grace of
> God—and all the more toward you.
>
> *—2 Corinthians 1:12*

Prayer:

O Eternal Light,
  I want to walk as a child of the light and to be filled with joy.
  I want a principle at the center of my being that not only
    represents who I am but is a guiding force that both
    accuses and excuses, disapproves and approves, condemns
    and acquits every thought, word, and deed from the
    perspective of your love.
  I need a conscience that helps me to perceive what is right
    and wrong, that helps me know how to live in loving
    relationships with other people.
  Grant to me, O Lord, a right understanding of your Word,
    a true understanding of my self, a consistency of heart and
    life, an inward perception that I walk in your ways and
    follow in your paths through faith in Jesus Christ.

Help me to cultivate a simplicity of spirit in my life—the
    ability to keep my eye firmly fixed upon Jesus in all things.
Nurture within me a godly sincerity, a daily reliance upon
    your strength, wisdom, and love,
    so that all of my conversation
    might be compelling and winsome and pure.
Witness to your love daily in my life through the power of
    your Spirit, so that I might rejoice in you always.
    May my joy—my happiness—always lead me
        to rejoice in obedience to your loving will,
        to rejoice in loving you,
        to rejoice in keeping your commandments.
    May my sense of blessedness spring from the assurance
        that you love me and have restored
        abundance to my life through Jesus Christ. Amen.

Hymn:

> I want a principle within
>   Of jealous, godly fear,
> A sensibility of sin,
>   A pain to feel it near.
>
> That I from thee no more may part,
>   No more thy goodness grieve,
> The filial awe, the fleshly heart,
>   The tender conscience give.
>
> Quick as the apple of an eye,
>   O God, my conscience make;
> Awake my soul when sin is nigh,
>   And keep it still awake.

(Collection 299:1-3)

13 ❧
Remaining Sin

Scripture:

> So if anyone is in Christ, there is a new creation.
>
> —*2 Corinthians 5:17*

Prayer:

Cleansing God,
   I want to be thoroughly clean, but I continue
      to struggle with sin,
      despite the fact that Jesus is the center of my life.
   I have to be honest about this.
   Although sin remains, I can say that
      it no longer controls my life as it once did.
So first and foremost, I want to thank you for freeing me from
   the control of all those forces that are contrary to the mind
   of Christ. To live in him is a great and glorious gift.
But two contrary principles are still at war in my life. While
   my spirit is willing, the flesh is weak. While I might appear
   to others to have been delivered from all those things that
   are unloving, I know my inner self all too well. I continue
   to struggle, Lord, to be wholly yours.
At times my heart is drawn away from your loving purpose
   and way. My spirit leans toward the unloving thought, the

unloving word. I am prone to turn away from you and to embrace those things I know to be wrong and harmful.

As long as I continue to fight against those things with the power to destroy my life, I know that you are with me and living in my heart. I want you to take complete control of every aspect of my life.

What a strange thing to be new and old at the same time, to be recreated by your love and yet continue to struggle with my old self.

You have freed me from the guilt and power of my own brokenness, but inner healing requires a long process of divine therapy.

While pride may rise up in my heart occasionally, deliver me from ever becoming a proud person.

While I may want to turn away from you from time to time, empower me to resist the strength of sin's attraction.

While darkness may appear to be strong in my life and in your world, may I ever feel safe and secure in your eternal light and love.

Renew me, cleanse me, purify my life, and restore me
in every possible way
in my love for you,
for the sake of Jesus Christ. Amen.

Hymn:

> Come, almighty to deliver,
>   Let us all thy grace receive;
> Suddenly return, and never,
>   Never more thy temples leave.
> Thee we would be always blessing,
>   Serve thee as thy hosts above,

Pray, and praise thee without ceasing,
   Glory in thy perfect love.

Finish then thy new creation,
   Pure and spotless let us be;
Let us see thy great salvation
   Perfectly restored in thee;
Changed from glory into glory,
   Till in heaven we take our place,
Till we cast our crowns before thee,
Lost in wonder, love, and praise.

(Collection 374:2, 3)

14 ❧
Continuing Repentance

Scripture:

> Repent, and believe in the good news.
>
> —*Mark 1:15*

Prayer:

Patient and Forgiving God,

    I need to ask your forgiveness for much, although I know I
        am your child. You have forgiven me for everything in
        Christ, but I continue to stumble and fall like a little child.

Christ reigns in my heart,

    but pride emerges in the shadow of my spiritual progress;
    self-will, idolatry, and love of the world assault my soul;
    desire and love of praise, jealousy, and envy crowd my
    thoughts. I feel terrible about the darkness remaining in
    my heart.

While my words and actions seem to be good and pure,

    my intentions and motives are sometimes self-serving and
        anything but godly. Sometimes I feel utterly helpless,
        and I know it is a a grand illusion to think I can expel
        pride, selfishness, and inbred sin on my own.

I trust you to deliver me from this sin that remains, just as you

    have freed me from the power of evil in my life. Not only

are you willing, you are able to liberate me fully. You want
me to grow from faith to faith and to feel the power of
Christ every moment.
In repentance I feel remaining sin; by faith I receive your
power to purify my heart and cleanse my hands.
In repentance I realize the consequences of my brokenness;
by faith I am conscious of Christ's pleading for me
and your liberating pardon.
In repentance I recognize my helplessness; by faith I accept
your mercy and experience your grace.
By your grace you free me from bondage to outward sin,
and the power of inward sin is broken while not entirely
destroyed.
When you accepted me as a part of your family through
Christ, I felt as though I was born again. The change in my
life was amazing.
But I need to experience your life-changing love over and
over again in order to grow into the fullness
of your love. Amen.

Hymn:

Saviour, Prince enthroned above,
Repentance to impart
Give me, through thy dying love,
The humble, contrite heart;
Give what I have long implored,
A portion of thy grief unknown;
Turn, and look upon me, Lord,
And break my heart of stone.

Look, as when thy languid eye
    Was closed that we might live;
'Father' (at the point to die
    My Saviour gasped), 'forgive!'
Surely with that dying word
He turns, and looks, and cries, "'Tis done!'
  O my bleeding, loving Lord,
    Thou break'st my heart of stone!

(Collection 103:2, 8)

15 ✎
The Great Judgment

Scripture:

> For we will all stand before the judgment seat of God.
>
> —*Romans 14:10*

Prayer:

Judge of all people,

How easy it is to live our lives without any thought to your judgment. But if we thought seriously about your "Day," O Lord, how much more we would strive for nobility in our character and love in our lives.

When we realize that Christ will be our judge and that each of us will be required to give an account of our lives—that the very thoughts and intentions of our hearts will be revealed—we know how important it is to rest in your arms and put our whole trust in Christ.

When that day comes, we pray to hear those words, "Come, blessed of my Father." Enable us to rejoice with overwhelming joy in that moment, not because of what we have done for you but because of what Christ has done for us.

We ask you not to remember our failures but to reveal your own glory and the magnitude of your forgiveness and love.

As the heavens pass away and everything is changed and all
things are drawn up into the mystery of your love, allow us
to find a place in the new heaven and the new earth, where
all language fails for the joy of the most perfect happiness
we can conceive.
While we remain in this world, give us courage
to defend the injured
and to work for justice and peace for all.
Fill us with your Spirit
to the extent that we burn with love for you
and all humanity.
Empower us to do justly and to love mercy.
We give ourselves to you who gave yourself for us, in
humble faith and holy, active, patient love. Amen.

Hymn:

Hearken to the solemn voice,
The awful midnight cry!
Waiting souls, rejoice, rejoice,
And see the bridegroom nigh!
Lo! he comes to keep his word;
Light and joy his looks impart;
Go ye forth to meet your Lord,
And meet him in your heart.

Happy he whom Christ shall find
Watching to see him come;
Him the Judge of all mankind
Shall bear triumphant home;
Who can answer to his word?

Which of you dares meet his day?
'Rise, and come to Judgment'—Lord,
We rise, and come away.

(Collection 53:1, 5)

16 ❧
Means of Grace

Scripture:

> You have turned aside from my statutes and have not
> kept them.
>
> —*Malachi 3:7*

Prayer:

Gracious and Loving God,

You seek us all and meet us in so many ways because you
long to share your love with everything and everyone
you have created.

We all need a vital, inward religion—a living relationship
with you—but we also know you reach out to us and
sustain us in your love in outward ways.

The places you have promised to meet us as your friends and
children—the ordinary means of grace—are prayer,
scripture, and the Lord's Supper.

In these gifts—these sign-acts of your love—you offer yourself
to us anew.

All who desire your grace are to wait for it by immersing
themselves in these means you have graciously offered
to us.

Lord, help us to wait for you in the way of prayer.

In prayer we realize your wonderful promises for all your
children.
Here you nurture our life of faith and build our trust
in you.
Lord, help us to wait for you in searching the scriptures.
As we hear, read, and meditate upon your Word, confirm
your truth, increase our wisdom, empower us to share
the fullness of Christ.
Lord, help us to wait for you as we share together in the
Lord's Supper.
Here your Word becomes real in our lives.
Here your love becomes visible and tangible and touches
us most deeply.
Guard us from trusting in these means rather than seeking
your presence,
from making your own means, ends in themselves.
Establish in our lives a consistent pattern that moves
from hearing, reading, and meditating upon your Word
to communicating our deepest feelings and needs to you
in prayer
to enjoying the presence of your company and
companionship in our fellowship
around your table.
You come to us, gracious God, in so many ways to bless us
and to make us whole and to show us your love.
Help us to look forward to being with you as our dearest
friend in all these ways. When we are with you, enable us
to abide in your presence and to rejoice in your love as the
most important reality of our lives. Amen.

Hymn:

> Fasting He doth, and hearing bless,
>> And prayer can much avail,
> Good vessels all to draw the grace
>> Out of salvation's well.
>
> But none, like this mysterious rite
>> Which dying mercy gave,
> Can draw forth all His promised might
>> And all His will to save.
>
> This is the richest legacy
>> Thou hast on man bestow'd:
> Here chiefly, Lord, we feed on Thee,
>> And drink Thy precious blood.

(HLS 42:2-4)

17 ❧
A Heart for God

> Real circumcision is a matter of the heart—it is spiritual
> and not literal.
>
> —*Romans 2:29*

Prayer:

God of my hopes and dreams,
  If I am going to live my life for you and your glory alone,
    I must die to all of those forces surrounding me
      that demean life and make it less than you have intended
        it to be.
  To be a true follower of Christ, my soul and mind and spirit
    need to be renewed, so I can become more like him.
  If I am to be renewed by your love, then you must transform
    my heart;
      you must change my hopes and dreams.
    Therefore, make me humble, Lord.
      Enable me to think rightly about myself.
        Remind me daily of my total dependence upon you,
          your grace and mercy in my life.
      Gift me with a solid faith that is mighty because it is
        rooted in you.

Deliver me from the power of sin and strengthen me
against temptation through the revelation of Christ in
my heart.
Plant the seed of hope in the center of my spirit.
And to humility, faith, and hope, add the most important
thing—love.
Direct every desire, thought, word, and action toward
your will.
May I have no other end in sight—no cherished hope
or dream—other than a loving relationship
with you.
You exalted Jesus because he humbled himself, and you
gave him a name above all other names. I pray that my
life of self-sacrificing love—patterned after his own—
might be an act of praise worthy of his honor.
Give me courage to build my life on this foundation, and
this foundation only—that of Christ who emptied
himself of everything but love.
Bear witness with my humble spirit then that I am
your true child.
Through self-denial and freely offered love to others,
help me to find my life by giving it away and thereby
experience the joy of the promises you make to all
your children.
As I fight the good fight of faith, transform my heart with your
love, I pray. Amen.

Hymn:

Thou, O Christ, art all I want,
more than all in thee I find;
raise the fallen, cheer the faint,

heal the sick, and lead the blind.
Just and holy is thy name,
 I am all unrighteousness;
false and full of sin I am;
 thou art full of truth and grace.

Plenteous grace with thee is found,
 grace to cover all my sin;
let the healing streams abound,
 make and keep me pure within.
Thou of life the fountain art,
 freely let me take of thee;
spring thou up within my heart;
 rise to all eternity!

(UMH 479:3, 4)

18 ❧
Marks of New Birth

Scripture:

So it is with everyone who is born of the Spirit.

—John 3:8

Prayer:

God of new beginnings,

I want to be born again. I want to be a new person, changed
by your love.

Mark my life, O gracious God, with *faith.*

Give me a faith that not only affirms your truth but
changes my heart, so that I rely alone on your mercy
and grace in Jesus Christ. And as a fruit of this faith, give
me power over sin and peace of heart and mind.

Mark my life, O radiant God, with *hope.*

Give me a hope that assures me when I walk in simplicity
and sincerity with you, a hope that bears witness to my
spirit that I am your child and a joint heir with Christ of
all the promises of your love. May all my sorrow be
melted into joy by your constant companionship.

Mark my life, O compassionate God, with *love.*

Give me a love for you that looks to you for all things and
enjoys your friendship. Help me to love Jesus. Empower

me to be loving to my neighbor. Enable me to obey the highest law of all—to have a heart so in tune with your heart that I always want to obey your universal law of love.

O God whose love is ever new, sweeping into our lives wherever and whenever it will, do not allow me to rest on actions, experiences, and memories in my past; rather birth me anew in the Spirit this very day and assure me in the deepest part of my spirit that I am, even now, your child forever. Amen.

Hymn:

> Come, Holy Ghost, all-quick'ning fire,
> Come, and my hallowed heart inspire,
>   Sprinkled with the atoning blood;
> Now to my soul thyself reveal,
> Thy mighty working let me feel,
>   And know that I am born of God.
> . . . .
> Humble, and teachable, and mild,
> O may I, as a little child,
>   My lowly Master's steps pursue!
> Be anger to my soul unknown;
> Hate, envy, jealousy, be gone!
>   In love create thou all things new.
>
> *(Collection 341:1, 2)*

19 🐾
Christian Privileges

Scripture:

> Those who have been born of God do not sin.
>
> —1 John 3:9

Prayer:

Holy and Life-giving God,

You change our relationship with you not only when you pardon our sin; more importantly, you heal our brokenness and change our lives from the inside out. You give us a new start, a new birth through the power of your Spirit indwelling our lives. Not only do you work *for* us, doing what we could never do for ourselves—removing our sense of guilt and shame—but you work *in* us, healing our broken hearts and restoring our souls. You offer to us the possibility of real change.

We need to be born again, O God, and you are the only one to offer us this gift. We need a spiritual birth similar to the gift of physical birth given to us by our mothers. This new birth must be not only an outward, visible miracle but a vast, inward change as well.

A child at birth becomes aware of a whole new world.

Birth us into your new world of love and care so that we

might sense and feel your presence in our lives. Open our eyes so that we might see and experience your love, mercy, reconciliation, pardon, and promise. Open our ears so that we might hear your voice and obey your call to be your faithful children.

Having been born again, conquering Lord, keep us from all sin. Guard us from intentionally turning our back on you and doing what we know is contrary to your way of love. Keep our intentions pure. Give us the courage we need to turn a deaf ear to those voices in our head that prompt us to act as anything less than your beloved children.

Plant the seed of loving, conquering faith deep in our soul. When temptation arises, warn us inwardly of the danger that is near, grieve our spirit, reprove us when we nurture the thought of turning away from you, and strengthen our resolve, so that evil will never have a chance to spread in our soul while faith and love vanish altogether.

Inspire us continually, O Lord, with your Holy Spirit.

Breathe into our soul that we might have abundant life in Christ.

Remind us to practice your presence daily in our life and long to be with you as much as we would cherish the company of our closest friend. Amen.

Hymn:

> From th'oppressive power of sin
> My struggling spirit free;
> Perfect righteousness bring in,
> Unspotted purity;

Speak, and all this war shall cease,
And sin shall give its raging o'er;
    Love me freely, seal my peace,
    And bid me sin no more.

For this only thing I pray,
    And this will I require—
Take the power of sin away,
    Fill me with chaste desire,
Perfect me in holiness,
Thine image to my soul restore;
    Love me freely, seal my peace,
    And bid me sin no more.

(Collection 106:5, 6)

20 ✒
The Righteousness of Christ

Scripture:

> And this is the name by which he will be called: "The
> Lord is our righteousness."
>
> —*Jeremiah 23:6*

Prayer:

We worship you, O God, because you are righteous and holy.
> We see your glory already in the face of Jesus Christ our Lord.
>> In his divinity we see your eternal, essential, and
>> unchanging holiness,
>>> your justice, mercy, and truth.
>> In his humanity we see not only his sinlessness and purity
>>> but also his complete obedience to your will, his
>>>> uncompromising life of compassion and self-
>>>> emptying love.
> You offer the fullness of who he is to us as a gift,
>> even though none of us deserves such a treasure.
> You forgive us and accept us wholly for the sake of what
>> Christ has done for us.
> Whenever we truly come to ourselves and believe the good
>> news of your love for us, it is as if we become like Christ in
>> your eyes. In that moment we know the absolute ecstasy

and liberation of being forgiven and accepted by you.
The wonders of your love for us do not stop there.
Not only do you call us your own children in Christ,
you also begin to make us truly gracious,
compassionate, and loving,
through the power of the Spirit at work within us.
The Spirit transforms and reshapes our lives to the very
image of our Lord.
We simply long to rest in Jesus and that suffices.
He became what we are in order for us to become what he
himself is, the embodiment of your love.
So clothe us with Christ, we pray, and transform the
brokenness of our humanity into the
holiness of your divine love. Amen.

Hymn:

O let thy Spirit shed abroad
The love, the perfect love of God
In this cold heart of mine!
O might he now descend, and rest,
And dwell for ever in my breast,
And make it all divine!

Take the dear purchase of thy blood,
My Friend and Advocate with God,
My ransom and my peace,
Surety, who all my debt hast paid,
For all my sins atonement made,
The Lord my righteousness!

(Collection 139:3, 5)

21 ✍

Yearning for God

Scripture:

> When Jesus saw the crowds, he went up the mountain;
> and after he sat down, his disciples came to him. Then he
> began to speak, and taught them, saying: "Blessed are the
> poor in spirit, for theirs is the kingdom of heaven. Blessed
> are those who mourn, for they will be comforted."
>
> —*Matthew 5:1-4*

Prayer:

Lord Jesus, Teacher of us all,
> Whenever I turn to your great Sermon on the Mount, I am
> > struck with awe
> > by the simplicity and profundity of your teaching.
You show us the way to fullness of life here and life
> > everlasting with God. Your words penetrate directly into
> > the hearts of all people, teaching as no other has ever
> > taught.
You reveal God's will, not with thunder or fire
> > but with amazing love,
> > > telling us what true religion is meant to be and how we
> > > > can live it out.
"Blessed are the poor in spirit," you proclaim, "for they are all

participants in the Reign of God."*
Poverty of spirit is the first step to all real, substantial
  happiness.
I know that to be poor in spirit means to acknowledge my
  brokenness and my helplessness. Much more than a
  superficial kind of humility, this poverty of spirit
  requires me to face myself with honesty, to renounce all
  of those forces that push me away from you, and to
  place all of my hope—my very life—into your hands.
But glory be to your name, for whenever I have found the
  courage and strength to be poor in spirit, I have
  experienced the birth of your reign in my heart anew.
  With your reign come
righteousness—your life and love in my very soul,
      the mind of Christ, and your image renewed;
  peace—a calm serenity of the soul;
  and joy in the Holy Spirit—the sealing of your promise
      in the depths of my heart.
I want to grow into this lowliness of heart, O God. I yearn
  for genuine Christian humility that flows from a deep
  sense of your love.
"Blessed are those who mourn," you add, "for they will be
  comforted."
O Jesus, you know us so well—you know me so well. You
  know how much pain I feel because of my brokenness
  and the many losses in my life—crushed hopes and
  abandoned dreams. They are all little deaths that cry
  out for healing.
You know as well that the deepest ache of my life is my
  yearning for you and the real happiness found in
  relationships rooted in your love. You know the agony
  that I feel when it seems I have been abandoned by my

friends and even God. You offer the promise of lifted
clouds and the overwhelming joy of God's shining face.
I mourn as well, compassionate Lord, for those around me
who have lost their way and are trapped in cycles of
misery and sin. Whenever we yearn for you and
rediscover our true selves through genuine humility,
allow your presence to shine in our lives and to draw all
into your loving family. Amen.

Hymn:

Jesu, if still the same thou art,
    If all thy promises are sure,
Set up thy kingdom in my heart,
    And make me rich, for I am poor:
To me be all thy treasures given,
The kingdom of an inward heaven.

Thou hast pronounced the mourners blest,
    And lo! for thee I ever mourn.
I cannot, no, I will not rest
    Till thou my only rest return;
Till thou, the Prince of peace, appear,
And I receive the Comforter.

(Collection 130:1, 2)

*Author's paraphrase

22 ✍

Meekness, Justice, and Mercy

Scripture:

> Blessed are the meek, for they will inherit the earth.
> Blessed are those who hunger and thirst for righteous-
> ness, for they will be filled. Blessed are the merciful, for
> they will receive mercy.
>
> *—Matthew 5:5-7*

Prayer:

Lord, I want to be *meek*—
    not apathetic about life or lacking in self-confidence—
    rather always resigned to your will and never demanding my
        own way,
    always patient and content in myself, at ease and at peace,
    always mild and gentle toward friends and enemies alike.
    I want to have a deep, interior meekness,
        not just the outward form;
        I want a spirit that is easily reconciled with others.
    You have said that the meek will inherit the earth. Since the
        meek fix their hearts, desires, and joys in you, they are
        happy in all things.
    Lord, I want to be meek.
Lord, I want to hunger and thirst for what is *right*.

If I am truly meek—
  if I allow you to heal my inner feelings of anger,
    impatience, and discontent—
  then I will desire healthy, honorable, and true
    relationships.
  Hunger and thirst are the strongest of all appetites. If I
    hunger and thirst for you, nothing will satisfy me except
    the blessings of your goodness and love. I want to be
    able to love as you love, to have the heart and mind that
    I see in Jesus Christ.
  Fill me then with the power of godliness—not just its
    outward signs—and never let the desire for your truth,
    justice, and beauty grow cold in me.
  Lord, I want to hunger and thirst for what is right.
Lord, I want to be *merciful.* If I am filled with your truth and
  goodness,
    then I will be tender toward those who do not know you
      and truly merciful,
    which means nothing other than loving my neighbor as I
      love myself.
  Lord, I want to be more loving in my heart:
    I want a love that is long-suffering, soft, and mild,
      a love that does not envy and is not hasty in judgment
        but humble,
      a love that is neither rude nor offensive
        but looks to the others' good,
      a love that is not easily provoked
        and never rejoices in evil
          but leaps for joy wherever it finds the truth and only
            speaks well of others.
    Lord, I want you to restore in me a love that is always ready
      to think the best, to transform the most evil designs of

others into hope-filled victories, and to endure injustice
and cruelty with a Christlike spirit of forgiveness.
Lord, I want to be merciful, and I hope against hope
because I know it is your good pleasure to renew not
only me but also the face of the whole earth. Amen.

Hymn:

Where is the blessedness bestowed
On all that hunger after thee?
I hunger now, I thirst for God!
See the poor fainting sinner, see,
And satisfy with endless peace,
And fill me with thy righteousness.

Lord, I believe the promise sure,
And trust thou wilt not long delay;
Hungry, and sorrowful, and poor,
Upon thy word myself I stay;
Into thine hands my all resign,
And wait till all thou art is mine!

(Collection 130:3, 6)

23 ✌

Purity, Peacemaking, and Reconciliation

Scripture:

> Blessed are the pure in heart, for they will see God.
> Blessed are the peacemakers, for they will be called chil-
> dren of God. Blessed are those who are persecuted for
> righteousness' sake, for theirs is the kingdom of heaven.
> Blessed are you when people revile you and persecute
> you and utter all kinds of evil against you falsely on my
> account. Rejoice and be glad, for your reward is great in
> heaven, for in the same way they persecuted the prophets
> who were before you.
>
> —*Matthew 5:8-12*

Prayer:

Holy God,

I know that purity of heart is the only true foundation of my
love for you and the love of my neighbor. Purify my heart
so that all my inward and outward affections are turned
toward you and your ways.

Enable me to discern your providential care, to perceive
your presence in all things, to think and feel and act as a
child of a living God. *Lord, purify my heart* that my life
might reflect your own pure love.

You have called me to be a peacemaker. The desire to reconcile and to be reconciled is a primary characteristic of your true children.

While you call me to *be* pure, you also call me to *do* those things that make for peace. Create a new spirit within me that detests all strife and contentious debate, all useless discord and violence. May I rejoice in every opportunity to do good to others.

Lord, pacify my heart that my life might reflect your peace.

Prepare me to face persecution with courage, Lord. All who identify themselves with your love and truth and justice will encounter hard times in a world that opposes your holy and loving rule.

All who love you and love their neighbors as themselves are persecuted because they are poor in spirit, mourn, are meek, merciful, pure in heart, and offer healing in the midst of brokenness.

The powers of evil in life wage war against the beauty of your love and oppose it at every possible opportunity. Those whose lives are dark do not merely pretend to hate your children, while actually admiring them; they truly hate them because they cannot endure the transforming power of your love.

When I am persecuted for your sake, Lord, give me the strength never to turn away from love and understanding and compassion. Enable me, through your grace, to love my enemies, to bless them that curse you, to do good to all who hate you, and to pray for them continually.

Lord, perfect my heart and life in this genuine religion of Jesus Christ! Amen.

Hymn:

> God of all-sufficient grace,
>   My God in Christ thou art;
> Bid me walk before thy face
>   Till I am pure in heart;
> Till, transformed by faith divine,
> I gain that perfect love unknown,
>   Bright in all thy image shine,
>   By putting on thy Son.
>
> Father, Son, and Holy Ghost,
>   In council join again
> To restore thine image, lost
>   By frail, apostate man;
> O might I thy form express,
> Through faith begotten from above,
>   Stamped with real holiness,
>   And filled with perfect love!

(Collection 357:3, 4)

24 🖎
Heart and Life

Scripture:

> You are the salt of the earth; but if salt has lost its taste,
> how can its saltiness be restored? It is no longer good for
> anything, but is thrown out and trampled under foot.
> You are the light of the world. A city built on a hill cannot
> be hid. No one after lighting a lamp puts it under the
> bushel basket, but on the lampstand, and it gives light to
> all in the house. In the same way, let your light shine
> before others, so that they may see your good works and
> give glory to your Father in heaven.
>
> —*Matthew 5:13-16*

Prayer:

God Made Visible in Jesus,

> You call me to a life of faith rooted in the heart but expressed
> in life. True religion is essentially social religion, and to
> turn it into a solitary religion—a religion of the heart
> only—is to destroy it.
> You call me to immerse myself in, not to separate myself
> from, your world.
> You call me to be like salt in the world and through my
> meekness, commitment to peace, and humility to flavor

life with your love.

Without immersing myself in and influencing the lives of others, I can never be the force for good that you so long for me to be.

How can I possibly conceal the beautiful light you have caused to shine in my heart? While some may be offended by that light, I will guard it carefully and pray that it may never be put out.

When others say that I should keep my religion to myself, that it is a private matter between you and me and should not be shown outwardly, remind me that the root and the branches are inseparable. The root must put forth branches if it is to live.

When others say that I can love without putting that love into action, remind me that love fulfills your law not by releasing us from the law but by compelling us to obey it.

When others say that love alone is the more excellent way, remind me that you have joined together the loving heart and outward works.

When others say that worshiping you in spirit is enough, remind me that to worship you in spirit and in truth means to glorify you by keeping your commandments with my body and my spirit.

When others say that outward works are useless and that trying to do good is pointless, remind me that you have commanded us to feed the hungry and care for the needy, not as means to obtain your love but as the fruit of a living faith in Christ.

I will let my light shine for you, O God. My only desire is to glorify you in all that I do. I will let my light shine for you in all good works of piety, in works of mercy, and by living simply that others might simply live. Amen.

Hymn:

> Jesus, let all thy lovers shine,
>> Illustrious as the sun;
> And bright with borrowed rays divine
>> Their glorious circuit run.

> As the great Sun of Righteousness
>> Their healing wings display,
> And let their lustre still increase
>> Unto the perfect day.

(Collection 434:3, 6)

25 ❧
Law and Gospel

Scripture:

> Do not think that I have come to abolish the law or the
> prophets; I have come not to abolish but to fulfill. For
> truly I tell you, until heaven and earth pass away, not one
> letter, not one stroke of a letter, will pass from the law
> until all is accomplished. Therefore, whoever breaks one
> of the least of these commandments, and teaches others
> to do the same, will be called least in the kingdom of
> heaven; but whoever does them and teaches them will be
> called great in the kingdom of heaven. For I tell you,
> unless your righteousness exceeds that of the scribes and
> Pharisees, you will never enter the kingdom of heaven.
>
> —*Matthew 5:17-20*

Prayer:

Loving and Righteous God,
> You call us to be loving people who do not abandon your law
> but are obedient to it because it is rooted in your love.
> Ceremonies and rituals pass away, but your law of love, O
> God, stands forever.
> Your grace and your law—the good news of your love for us
> in Christ and your demand for justice—are not two

separate things but one and the same expression of your
will for all people. Your law continually points to the
gospel, and the gospel continually leads us to a more exact
fulfilling of your law.
Guard us from failing to recognize this important connection,
from willfully disregarding your loving directions for life,
from emphasizing the inner life while ignoring the
external demands for justice,
and from believing we are above your law because we have
been saved by your grace.
What we need is a faith that works by love.
Guard us from the trap of being religious but never living in
your Spirit,
from trusting ourselves to measure up to the highest
standard of your law of love.
Empower us through our faith
to be great in our capacity to love, rather than falsely
viewing ourselves as better than others;
to immerse ourselves in your means of grace, not to show
off but to learn how to be more loving and
compassionate to others;
to give with glad and generous hearts, not to feel good
about ourselves but to offer all we have for others.
By the power of your love at work within us, enable us to
fulfill not only the letter but more particularly the spirit of
the law,
that you might be glorified in all things
and that our transparent love for you and our neighbor
might point to your purity, justice, and love. Amen.

Hymn:

> That blessed law of thine,
>   Jesu, to me impart:
> Thy Spirit's law of life divine,
>   O write it in my heart!
>   Implant it deep within,
>   Whence it may ne'er remove,
> The law of liberty from sin,
>   The perfect law of love.
>
>   Thy nature be my law,
>   Thy spotless sanctity,
> And sweetly every moment draw
>   My happy soul to thee!
>   Soul of my soul remain!
>   Who didst for all fulfil,
> In me, O Lord, fulfil again
>   Thy heavenly Father's will!

(Collection 331:2, 3)

26 ☙
The Lord's Prayer

Beware of practicing your piety before others in order to be seen by them; for then you have no reward from your Father in heaven.

So whenever you give alms, do not sound a trumpet before you, as the hypocrites do in the synagogues and in the streets, so that they may be praised by others. Truly I tell you, they have received their reward. But when you give alms, do not let your left hand know what your right hand is doing, so that your alms may be done in secret; and your Father who sees in secret will reward you.

And whenever you pray, do not be like the hypocrites; for they love to stand and pray in the synagogues and at the street corners, so that they may be seen by others. Truly I tell you, they have received their reward. But whenever you pray, go into your room and shut the door and pray to your Father who is in secret; and your Father who sees in secret will reward you.

When you are praying, do not heap up empty phrases as the Gentiles do; for they think that they will be heard because of their many words. Do not be like them, for your Father knows what you need before you ask him. Pray then in this way:

Our Father in heaven,
    hallowed be your name.
    Your kingdom come.
    Your will be done,
        on earth as it is in heaven.
    Give us this day our daily bread.
    And forgive us our debts,
        as we also have forgiven our debtors.
    And do not bring us to the time of trial,
        but rescue us from the evil one.
For if you forgive others their trespasses, your heavenly
Father will also forgive you; but if you do not forgive
others, neither will your Father forgive your trespasses.

—Matthew 6:1-15

Prayer:

Abba, Father,

If my intention is pure and holy, then all of my actions will
    spring from a heart centered in you. Create a new and
    clean heart within me then, O God, so that I might have a
    right motivation in all my acts of devotion and works of
    compassion.

When I feed the hungry, clothe the naked, assist the stranger,
    and visit the sick, may I be guided in my actions by your
    genuine love.

When I pray, enable me to open my heart to you with true
    sincerity and open my life to your transforming power in
    humility and trust.

May all my prayers be modeled after Jesus' prayer, which is the
    fullest expression of all my needs, my deepest desires, and
    my yearning to offer back to you all that I am.

"Our Father in heaven"—you are good and loving to me and only wish the very best for me in my life. You are my Creator, my Preserver, the Father of my Lord, Jesus Christ. You call me into a family to share your love. High and lifted up, you are God over all.

"Hallowed be your name"—you are eternal, all-knowing, all-wise, three-in-one and one-in-three, purity and holiness, love that knows no bounds.

"Your kingdom come"—come in a personal way to all who repent and believe and set up your peaceful reign in our hearts.

"Your will be done, on earth as it is in heaven"—conform our wills to your own loving will, that we might continually and perfectly be shaped by your love in every possible way and bring the whole world to a knowledge of your mercy and grace.

"Give us this day our daily bread"—provide for us all of those things which we need to grow as your children, both in our bodies and our spirits, for we make no claim to be able to feed ourselves properly, and we trust in your great mercies to us.

"And forgive us our debts, as we also have forgiven our debtors"—liberate us from the burden of our sins, unloose our chains, and help us to see that the healing of our own spirits is intimately connected with our willingness to offer healing to others.

"And do not bring us to the time of trial, but rescue us from the evil one"—guard us from events in life that separate us from a sense of your presence and protect us from all those forces that cause us to turn our backs on you.

You are God! We praise you!

You are the Lord! We acclaim you!

All creation worships you! Glory be to your name now and
for ever. Amen.

Hymn:

> Father of all, whose powerful voice
>   Called forth this universal frame,
> Whose mercies over all rejoice,
>   Through endless ages still the same;
> Thou by thy word upholdest all;
>   Thy bounteous love to all is showed;
> Thou hear'st thy every creature's call,
>   And fillest every mouth with good.
>
> Blessing, and honour, praise, and love,
>   Co-equal, co-eternal Three,
> In earth below, and heaven above,
>   By all thy works be paid to thee.
> Thrice holy, thine the kingdom is,
>   The power omnipotent is thine;
> And when created nature dies
>   Thy never-ceasing glories shine.

(Collection 225:1; 227:3)

27 ❧
Fasting

Scripture:

> And whenever you fast, do not look dismal, like the
> hypocrites, for they disfigure their faces so as to show
> others that they are fasting. Truly I tell you, they have
> received their reward. But when you fast, put oil on your
> head and wash your face, so that your fasting may be seen
> not by others but by your Father who is in secret; and
> your Father who sees in secret will reward you.
>
> —*Matthew 6:16-18*

Prayer:

Blessed God,

Your witness to us in scripture is filled with allusions to
fasting, and I know that this spiritual discipline is closely
connected to prayer.

I know that fasting is much more than simply abstaining
from food for one day or parts of days or on special days.
Fasting is an attitude, a discipline of the spirit; it has to do
with my longing to be closer to you, my dearest friend.

When I am overwhelmed by sorrow because of the
hurtfulness of my words and actions, fasting can be the
food for my healing.

When I have fallen into a pattern of overeating and have
   harmed my own health because of it, fasting can remind
   me that food is a gift and my body, your temple.
When foolish and hurtful desires well up within me, fasting
   can refocus my energies and my life on what is truly noble.
When I have abused your good gifts of any kind, fasting can
   restore a proper perspective toward your many blessings in
   my life.
When I am struggling in my life of prayer, fasting can draw me
   closer to you in my efforts to share my deepest longings
   and my heartfelt desires.
When I need to hear your voice, your corrective as well as your
   comforting words, fasting can open my ears to your still,
   small voice within.
When, in the midst of my blindness, you offer me a precious
   treasure to lift my soul, fasting can open my eyes to
   perceive your blessed presence in all things.
Certainly, it is important for me to fast, as it were, from
   sin, from pride, vanity, foolishness, and anger, but you
   also call me to discipline my spirit by self-denial, so that
   these unholy attitudes and actions cannot take root in
   my soul.
Teach me then, O Lord, how to fast in a proper way that will
   enable your loving spirit to shape and guide my life.
   Keep my heart and mind focused on you at all times.
   Remind me that fasting is a means to an end, not an end
      in itself.
   Enable me to be attentive to the inward and spiritual gift.
   Guard me from extremes that drive love out of my efforts
      to draw closer to you.
   Empower me to pray much and to translate my self-
      discipline into acts of kindness and mercy to others.

When I fast, O Lord, come to me in all the fullness of your love. Change my heart; clean up my life; conform me completely to your will and to your way; make me zealous to glorify you and offer myself up to you anew for your service. Above all else, make me more loving. Amen.

Hymn:

> O hide this self from me, that I
> No more, but Christ in me may live!
> My vile affections crucify,
> Nor let one darling lust survive.
> In all things nothing may I see,
> Nothing desire or seek but thee.
>
> Each moment draw from earth away
> My heart, that lowly waits thy call;
> Speak to my inmost soul and say,
> 'I am thy love, thy God, thy all!'
> To feel thy power, to hear thy voice,
> To taste thy love, be all my choice.

(Collection 335:5, 8)

28 ❧
Christian Treasure

Scripture:

> Do not store up for yourselves treasures on earth, where
> moth and rust consume and where thieves break in and
> steal; but store up for yourselves treasures in heaven,
> where neither moth nor rust consumes and where thieves
> do not break in and steal. For where your treasure is,
> there your heart will be also.
>
> The eye is the lamp of the body. So, if your eye is
> healthy, your whole body will be full of light; but if your
> eye is unhealthy, your whole body will be full of dark-
> ness. If then the light in you is darkness, how great is the
> darkness!
>
> —*Matthew 6:19-23*

Prayer:

Joyful and Giving God,
  You rejoice in the child whose eye is focused on you alone.
  What the eye is to the body, the intention is to the soul. So if
    my spirit is focused on knowing you and following Jesus
    Christ in all things, then my life will be filled with light:
    the light of holiness, being filled with love for you and love
      for all my brothers and sisters in the human family,

and the light of happiness, rejoicing in all things and
   giving thanks for all the blessings of life.
Guard me, therefore, from infatuation with what the world
   says I must have.
Give me enough to provide for myself and my family, but
   save me from the temptation to think I need more. Help
   me to realize how easily I can be led astray by worldly
   riches and how quickly they can take over my heart. It is
   very easy, indeed, for my possessions to own me, and for
   me to lose track of my most important love.
You are not concerned about my earthly riches;
   you esteem my integrity as a wonderful human being that
   you have created.
You do not call me to trust in my possessions for help
   or happiness.
You call me to put my trust in you, the source of all aid and
   blessedness in life.
Help me to renounce efforts to increase my own wealth.
   Rather let me improve the lives of other people by
   using what little I have wisely, for them and for the sake
   of Christ.
Give me courage to build reservoirs of spiritual treasure in my
   life, to strive in every way to be a faithful and wise steward
   of your gifts, and to live for you and for the poor. Amen.

Hymn:

   All my treasure is above;
   All my riches is thy love.
   Who the worth of love can tell?
   Infinite, unsearchable!

Thou, O love, my portion art.
Lord, thou know'st my simple heart:
Other comforts I despise—
Love be all my paradise.

Nothing else can I require;
Love fills up my whole desire.
All thy other gifts remove,
Still thou giv'st me all in love.

(Collection 422:5-7)

29 ✋
One Master

No one can serve two masters; for a slave will either hate
the one and love the other, or be devoted to the one and
despise the other. You cannot serve God and wealth.

Therefore I tell you, do not worry about your life,
what you will eat or what you will drink, or about your
body, what you will wear. Is not life more than food, and
the body more than clothing? Look at the birds of the air;
they neither sow nor reap nor gather into barns, and yet
your heavenly Father feeds them. Are you not of more
value than they? And can any of you by worrying add a
single hour to your span of life? And why do you worry
about clothing? Consider the lilies of the field, how they
grow; they neither toil nor spin, yet I tell you, even
Solomon in all his glory was not clothed like one of
these. But if God so clothes the grass of the field, which is
alive today and tomorrow is thrown into the oven, will
he not much more clothe you—you of little faith?
Therefore do not worry, saying, "What will we eat?" or
"What will we drink?" or "What will we wear?" For it is
the Gentiles who strive for all these things; and indeed
your heavenly Father knows that you need all these
things. But strive first for the kingdom of God and his

righteousness, and all these things will be given to
you as well.

So do not worry about tomorrow, for tomorrow
will bring worries of its own. Today's trouble is enough
for today.

—*Matthew 6:24-34*

Prayer:

O Lord and Master of All Humanity,
>   We cannot love you fully if our heart is divided. If we have
>   more than one master, we will always be pulled in
>   different directions.
>   To serve you and you alone is first and foremost
>   to believe in you,
>   to trust in you as our strength, help, shield, and defender,
>   to trust in you as our happiness,
>   to trust in you as the end toward which all of life moves.
>   To serve you also means to love you and you alone,
>   to love you as the one God,
>   to desire you alone for your own sake,
>   to rejoice and delight in you forever.
>   To serve you is to imitate you in our heart and life.
>   To serve you is to obey you by keeping your commandments
>   and to make the law of love the guiding force in our life.
>   Therefore, we will not trust in riches or love the world,
>   conforming our life to the values and standards of this age,
>   rather than being transformed by the power of your self-
>   giving love.
>   We will seek nothing but you, O God, and we will not worry
>   about our own life and what we need, for we know that
>   you will take care of us.

We will work hard to care for one another, but we will not allow concerns for the things of this world to take control of our life.

We will seek, above all else, the realization of your reign in our heart and the fruit of your love in our life, for we know that if we entrust our life to you and your ways, then you will provide all we need to be happy and contented in life.

We will live as in the light of eternity but keep our eyes focused upon the present and its actions, rather than upon the future and its dreams.

This day we will pursue nothing but love, serving and enjoying you, our one Lord and Master, in all things. Amen.

Hymn:

> Happy man whom God doth aid!
> God our souls and bodies made,
> God on us, in gracious showers,
> Blessings every moment pours,
> Compasses with angel-bands,
> Bids them bear us in their hands;
> Parents, friends, 'twas God bestowed,
> Life and all descends from God.
>
> He this flowery carpet spread,
> Made the earth on which we tread;
> God refreshes in the air,
> Covers with the clothes we wear,
> Feeds us with the food we eat,
> Cheers us by his light and heat,
> Makes his sun on us to shine—
> All our blessings are divine!

(Collection 223:1, 2)

30 🖎
The Loving Attitude

Scripture:

> Do not judge, so that you may not be judged. For with
> the judgment you make you will be judged, and the
> measure you give will be the measure you get.
>
> Why do you see the speck in your neighbor's eye, but
> do not notice the log in your own eye? Or how can you
> say to your neighbor, "Let me take the speck out of your
> eye," while the log is in your own eye? You hypocrite, first
> take the log out of your own eye, and then you will see
> clearly to take the speck out of your neighbor's eye.
>
> "Do not give what is holy to dogs; and do not throw
> your pearls before swine, or they will trample them under
> foot and turn and maul you.
>
> "Ask, and it will be given you; search, and you will
> find; knock, and the door will be opened for you. For
> everyone who asks receives, and everyone who searches
> finds, and for everyone who knocks, the door will be
> opened. Is there anyone among you who, if your child
> asks for bread, will give a stone? Or if the child asks for a
> fish, will give a snake? If you then, who are evil, know
> how to give good gifts to your children, how much more
> will your Father in heaven give good things to those who
> ask him!

"In everything do to others as you would have them
do to you; for this is the law and the prophets."

—*Matthew 7:1-12*

Prayer:

God of Justice and Love,

There is no greater barrier to our becoming the people you
want us to be than the temptation to judge others.

The most destructive judgmental attitude is thinking about
other people in any way contrary to your love:
to blame others when they are not responsible,
to condemn others for being wrong when they are not,
to discern a bad intention when it does not exist.

Guard us, Lord, from a spirit of condemnation that looks for
faults in other people and makes them feel guilty so that
we might feel better about ourselves. We know this spirit is
not loving.

If we believe that someone has strayed from your path, give us
courage to be honest and direct with that person, speaking
the truth in love but always leaving that person in your
hands.

When others turn their back on your good news of
forgiveness and love, help us to turn to prayer rather than
striking out at them. We know you will hear our prayers
and that they will be effective if our hearts are loving. Our
prayers will change us, and others will be transformed by
the power of your love that they see in us.

Your law of love is marvelously summed up in Jesus' words:
"In everything do to others as you would have them do to
you." We do not want others to judge us, so we must not
judge them. Our desire is for people to love and esteem us,

to act with justice, mercy, and truth toward us; so too then
we should act toward them.

This is what it means to be loving, O God. This is what leads
to blessedness in life and reconciliation in the midst of our
brokenness.

We praise you and give you thanks because we know that we
could never love in such a way unless you first loved us in
Christ and we loved him. His grace enables us to
relinquish judgmental attitudes and to be loving in all of
our relationships. Amen.

Hymn:

> Jesu, thine all-victorious love
> Shed in my heart abroad!
> Then shall my feet no longer rove,
> Rooted and fixed in God.
>
> Refining fire, go through my heart,
> Illuminate my soul;
> Scatter thy life through every part,
> And sanctify the whole.
>
> My steadfast soul, from falling free,
> Shall then no longer move;
> But Christ be all the world to me,
> And all my heart be love.

(Collection 351:4, 9, 12)

31 ❧
The Narrow Gate

Scripture:

> Enter through the narrow gate; for the gate is wide and
> the road is easy that leads to destruction, and there are
> many who take it. For the gate is narrow and the road is
> hard that leads to life, and there are few who find it.
>
> —*Matthew 7:13-14*

Prayer:

Guardian God,
I realize that the way that leads to eternal life is very narrow
   and that the way that leads to my destruction is very wide.
Sin is like a wide gate that is always easy to enter but leads
   only to brokenness and disaster for my life.
It often seems that every part of me is affected by my pride,
   self-will, lust, and love of the world. I place these
   parent-sins before my love of you.
But the rotten fruit produced by these disordered affections
   is as plentiful as grains of sand.
I don't want to walk in this way of destruction.
I want to be inwardly, as well as outwardly, changed.
   The way leading to blessedness is holiness of heart and life.
   So few travel this path, and the bad examples of those who

take the broad and destructive path are almost
overwhelming. To make it worse, I sometimes feel
persuaded to believe that the broad way is the right path to
follow. It sometimes seems that might and power are right,
and I am easily led astray.
But when I come to my senses, I realize that the rich and the
mighty only play on my fears in order to justify their own
perversions.
How ironic it is that the simple people of the narrow way are
discounted by the wise and powerful of this world. The
only argument of your true people is the nobility and
unselfish character of their lives.
O Holy God, give me courage to enter in at the straight and
narrow gate.
Transform my mind and my heart so that I might be completely
rooted and grounded in your love, for only the narrow path
of love will ultimately lead me home to you. Amen.

Hymn:

> Leader of faithful souls, and guide
>   Of all that travel to the sky,
> Come, and with us, even us abide,
>   Who would on thee alone rely;
> On thee alone our spirits stay,
> While held in life's uneven way.
>
> Raised by the breath of love divine,
>   We urge our way with strength renewed;
> The church of the first-born to join,
>   We travel to the mount of God;
> With joy upon our heads arise,
> And meet our Captain in the skies.

(Collection 69:1, 6)

32 ✒
False Teachers

Scripture:

> Beware of false prophets, who come to you in sheep's
> clothing but inwardly are ravenous wolves. You will
> know them by their fruits. Are grapes gathered from
> thorns, or figs from thistles? In the same way, every good
> tree bears good fruit, but the bad tree bears bad fruit. A
> good tree cannot bear bad fruit, nor can a bad tree bear
> good fruit. Every tree that does not bear good fruit is cut
> down and thrown into the fire. Thus you will know them
> by their fruits.
>
> —*Matthew 7:15-20*

Prayer:

God of Truth and Light,

> We live in a time of false teachers, men and women who
> claim to speak on your behalf and for the sake of love, but
> who, in fact, have exchanged your truth for lies.

> Guard your faithful people against those who teach a false
> way to heaven and do not teach the truth.

> If we encounter those who say that anything but humility,
> meekness, holy desire, love of you and neighbor, doing
> good and suffering for Christ is the loving way, enable us
> to discern the false message they proclaim.

Many in our world today teach the way of pride, passion, worldly desires, love of pleasure, unkindness, apathy, and indifference to holiness of heart and life, even in the life of your church. Help us to see that their hearts are not focused on you.

When wolves come to us in sheep's clothing, appearing to be harmless, religious, and loving, guard us against their evil intent and help us to perceive their subtle disguises.

Give us eyes to see the real fruit of their lives and not their empty promises.

Grant us wisdom to see through their methods of cheap grace: they are unable to truly change people's lives for the better. Instead they leave them in their sin and call their darkness light.

Empower us with your transforming love and keep us in your way.

Whenever they appeal to us to accept their distorted truths and ways of life, whether through false teaching about scripture or impassioned rationalizations for unholy living, enable us to wait upon you in prayer, and then to act accordingly, and always in love.

We ask you, O God, to purify the hearts and minds of those who have perverted your truth. We pray for the transformation of those who have taught a lie so long that they believe it themselves. Soften their hearts and open their eyes to the light of your truth! Amen.

Hymn:

> Into a world of ruffians sent,
>   I walk on hostile ground;
> Wild human bears on slaughter bent,
>   And ravening wolves surround.

But thou hast given a loud alarm,
 And thou shalt still prepare
My soul for all assaults, and arm
 With never-ceasing prayer.

O do not suffer me to sleep,
 Who on thy love depend,
But still thy faithful servant keep,
 And save me to the end.

(Collection 301:1, 5, 6)

33 🪶
A Secure Foundation

Scripture:

> Not everyone who says to me, "Lord, Lord," will enter the kingdom of heaven, but only the one who does the will of my Father in heaven. On that day many will say to me, "Lord, Lord, did we not prophesy in your name, and cast out demons in your name, and do many deeds of power in your name?" Then I will declare to them, "I never knew you; go away from me, you evildoers."
>
> Everyone then who hears these words of mine and acts on them will be like a wise man who built his house on rock. The rain fell, the floods came, and the winds blew and beat on that house, but it did not fall, because it had been founded on rock. And everyone who hears these words of mine and does not act on them will be like a foolish man who built his house on sand. The rain fell, and the floods came, and the winds blew and beat against that house, and it fell—and great was its fall.
>
> —*Matthew 7:21-27*

Prayer:

Faithful God,
   Your greatest desire for me is for me to be happy and holy,

and the only way to realize your dream for my life is to
build it on a secure foundation.
A house built upon the sand will quickly fall to the ground. I
could easily reduce religion to an external facade, empty
actions that have no meaning, simply trying to be good.
But this falls far short of true religion, which is a living
relationship with you through Jesus Christ. If I build my
life on any foundation other than that of your
unconditional love graciously received in your Son,
I build on sand.
Jesus is a rock, a sure foundation, upon which to build a life
worth living.
If I entrust my life to him, then I will want to do your will,
I will strive to fulfill the law of love in all things,
I will reflect his humility in my relationships with others,
I will seek to be patient, gentle, and meek,
and I will find the capacity to love you with all my heart.
If my relationship with you is strong because of the
indwelling Christ,
then I will know myself, even as you know me,
I will understand my place in your world as a pilgrim of
love,
and, most importantly, I will know you as my closest and
dearest friend.
Rooted in the love of Jesus and enlightened by your grace, I
will know that my purpose in life is to glorify you who
made me for yourself and to love and enjoy you forever!
This rock, this secure foundation, will never change or
founder.
So I ask myself, in prayer this day, upon which foundation
am I building my life? Have I built upon the foundation of
simply believing the right things, acting the right ways,

harming no one and doing good works, or attending the right church? Oh, these are the least part of the religion of Jesus Christ!

Or am I building my life on a dynamic and living relationship with you? Here is the foundation that will stand the test of time.

Add meekness of wisdom and contentment to my seriousness.

Enable me to love the sinner while speaking the truth in love.

Remove worldly desires for wealth, honors, and pleasures from my heart.

Empower me to love my neighbor just as I love myself and to be merciful and kind to everyone I meet.

Purify my heart and create a welcoming space there for you to reign forever. Amen.

Hymn:

How weak the thoughts and vain
Of self-deluding men!
Men, who fixed to earth alone
Think their houses shall endure,
Fondly call their lands their own,
To their distant heirs secure!

How happy then are we,
Who build, O Lord, on thee!
What can our foundation shock?
Though the shattered earth remove,
Stands our city on a rock,
On the rock of heavenly love.

(Collection 65:1, 2)

34 ❧
God's Law

Scripture:

> So the law is holy, and the commandment is holy and
> just and good.
>
> *—Romans 7:12*

Prayer:

Holy, Just, and Good God,
   Nothing could be more important in our lives than to
      understand and obey your law, for it is the source of
      life for those who believe.
   You gave us the law originally as a complete model of all truth
      and wove it into the very fabric of our lives. We rebelled
      against you, and in turning away from you we lost the true
      light of your law of love. You chose a particular people to
      whom you gave a more perfect knowledge of your rule of
      life and then, in Christ, established a new relationship
      with all your children so that we might have the law
      written on our hearts anew.
   Your law is a perfect picture of you for us. It is so much more
      than ceremonies and traditions. Your law is nothing less
      than your divine virtue and wisdom in a visible form. It is
      like a projection of your eternal mind, a transcript of
      your nature that we can easily read for ourselves. Most

importantly, the law is rooted in your love.

Your law, O God, is *holy.*

It is your wisdom from above: pure, chaste, clean, and
holy. It uncovers our brokenness and brings us to
our senses.

Your law, O God, is *just.*

It prescribes exactly what is best for everyone. It is the
unchangeable rule of right and wrong, willed and
created by you for the good of all.

Your law, O God, is *good.*

It was your goodness, your pure love, that led you to give
the law to us as a gift. It is like a fountain, therefore,
springing up, full of goodness and truth.

Lead us, good God, to know and use this gift in a proper way.

Convince us of our sin through your law, so that
we can be healed.

Transform us through your law, so that
we can truly live in Christ.

Sustain us through your law, so that
we can remain in you always.

Your Spirit will strengthen us in Christ, empower us to obey
your law of love, and confirm us in hope. Accept our
thanksgiving for the gift of your law which you have
written on our hearts anew in Christ, for it is perfect
freedom, the freedom of servant love. Amen.

Hymn:

> Father of all, in whom alone
>   We live, and move, and breathe,
> One bright celestial ray dart down,
>   And cheer thy sons beneath.
>
> While in thy Word we search for thee
>   (We search with trembling awe!)
> Open our eyes, and let us see
>   The wonders of thy law.
>
> Now let our darkness comprehend
>   The light that shines so clear;
> Now the revealing Spirit send,
>   And give us ears to hear.

(Collection 86:1-3)

35 ✍
Dishonoring God's Law

Scripture:

> Do we then overthrow the law by this faith? By no
> means! On the contrary, we uphold the law.
>
> —*Romans 3:31*

Prayer:

Gracious God,

You restore us to yourself by your gracious offer of new life in
Christ. Our grace-filled response of faith is all you ask. But
since our redemption is founded upon your grace and not
our good works, it is easy for us to abandon your law.

We dishonor your law by our failure to proclaim it as an
essential part of the Christian life, the fruit of a living faith.

No one made this more clear to us than your great Apostle
Paul. He not only declared the love of Christ to sinners
and their need to trust in Christ but also preached
about works so powerfully that no one could mistake
the necessity of living in obedience to your law.

You call us to declare both your promises
and your demands.

We dishonor your law by living as though faith is more
important than love.

While you restore us and heal our broken lives by the gift of faith, faith is a means to our actually becoming more loving people. It is not an end in itself, and to treat faith as the goal of life is to miss the point, the goal of love. The immediate fruit of a living faith ought to be our loving and reconciling actions toward others.

True holiness can never precede your gift of faith—we cannot live as your loving children without the prior experience of your love in our lives—but having experienced your unconditional love in Jesus, true holiness and happiness in life will surely follow.

We dishonor your law by living as if faith were designed to excuse us from holiness of heart and life.

Living "under your law" does not mean that we are obliged to observe special ceremonies, to conform to particular traditions, or to keep every commandment in order to deserve or win your love.

We are called to obey your law, gracious God, not because we fear you but because your love has filled our hearts to overflowing.

Empower us to honor and uphold your law of love, not because we fear the consequences of a broken, sinful life but because the gifts of grace, mercy, and faith have transformed us into a loving people. Amen.

Hymn:

> Jesu, thy boundless love to me
> No thought can reach, no tongue declare;
> O knit my thankful heart to thee,
> And reign without a rival there!
> Thine wholly, thine alone I am;
> Be thou alone my constant flame!

O grant that nothing in my soul
　　May dwell, but thy pure love alone!
O may thy love possess me whole,
　　My joy, my treasure, and my crown;
Strange flames far from my heart remove—
My every act, word, thought, be love.

(Collection 362:1, 2)

36 🐀
Honoring God's Law

Scripture:

> Do we then overthrow the law by this faith? By no
> means! On the contrary, we uphold the law.

—Romans 3:31

Prayer:

Guiding Light,

We honor your law by our belief in Christ and by offering
him to others.

Whenever we are plain and clear about your highest
standards concerning our lives, neither compromising
nor softening them,

whenever we declare both your law's absolute nature and
its spiritual meaning,

whenever we emphasize both outward actions and inward
attitudes, we honor your law and reveal what is
hidden from many.

Help us not only to proclaim everything you have
commanded but also to declare all the blessings and
privileges that you have prepared for your faithful
children. Our witness can awaken those who sleep,
instruct the ignorant, comfort the afflicted, and build

up our brothers and sisters in the faith.
We honor your law when we proclaim faith as the foundation
of love that leads to holiness of heart and life.
Faith, O God, is the means by which we become more
loving. But your love existed long before our faith, and
love will continue on long after faith has disappeared.
We honor your law when we allow it to take deep root in our
hearts and lives.
Without the law of love in our hearts, *nothing else matters.* It
is by our confidence and trust in your pardoning love
that you heal our broken hearts, and a sense of your
love for us in Christ is the most powerful motivation for
us to be a loving people.
Faith works inwardly by love to purify our hearts.
Empower us to honor and uphold your law of love by
opening our lives to the transforming presence of your
Spirit and by allowing us to walk daily in the radiant light
of Jesus, our Lord. Amen.

Hymn:

> Plead we thus for faith alone,
> Faith which by our works is shown;
> God it is who justifies,
> Only faith the grace applies,
> Active faith that lives within,
> Conquers earth, and hell, and sin,
> Sanctifies, and makes us whole,
> Forms the Saviour in the soul.
>
> Let us for this faith contend,
> Sure salvation is its end;

Heaven already is begun,
Everlasting life is won.
Only let us persevere
Till we see our Lord appear;
Never from the rock remove,
Saved by faith which works by love.

(Collection 507:3, 4)

37 ✒

The Nature of Enthusiasm

Scripture:

> While he was making this defense, Festus exclaimed,
> "You are out of your mind, Paul!"
>
> —*Acts 26:24*

Prayer:

O Fire of Love,

If I reject the values of this world and put my trust in
spiritual things,

if I rejoice in your loving embrace and love you above all,

if I celebrate the presence of your Holy Spirit in my life,

then people simply laugh at me and describe me as a
religious fanatic, an enthusiastic, nonconforming fool.

Despite all the good meanings of the word *enthusiasm,* it hurts
me deeply when others think that my faith is some kind of
mental disorder, some disease from which to recover, or at
best, childish foolishness I should outgrow.

I don't ever want to give anyone cause to call me a hypocrite. I
don't ever want my Christianity to be something in name
only, something based upon empty rituals, peculiar
opinions and traditions, or the simple fact that I live a
good life. I don't ever want to be an "imaginary Christian."

Neither do I want people to think that I consider myself to be particularly spiritual or more spiritual than others, as if they are not.

Neither do I expect you to guide me through visions or dreams or superstitious rites, when your Word stands forever as the true light for my path. The clear and ordinary way to know your will for my life is to live in your Word and to discern, as best I can, what leads to goodness and holiness and love.

I want to discipline myself in a life immersed in your means of grace, never believing that I can achieve any spiritual end by ignoring your means.

I want to affirm your care and concern for my life without becoming obsessed with discerning your activity in my life in a frivolous way.

Guard me, therefore, from judging others too harshly,
from falling into a dangerous kind of fanaticism that alienates others,
from condemning others rather than winning them by truth and love,
from thinking more highly of myself than I ought to think,
from failing to understand myself through your eyes.

Conform my life to that of the humble Christ and allow his Spirit to fill my soul in such a way that my enthusiasm is the fanaticism of love. Amen.

Hymn:

> Plant, and root, and fix in me
> All the mind that was in thee;
> Settled peace I then shall find—
> Jesu's is a quiet mind.

I shall nothing know beside
Jesus, and him crucified;
I shall all to him be joined—
Jesu's is a loving mind.

I shall triumph evermore,
Gratefully my God adore,
God so good, so true, so kind—
Jesu's is a thankful mind.

(Collection 345:5, 10, 11)

38 ❧
Caution against Bigotry

Scripture:

> John said to him, "Teacher, we saw someone casting out demons in your name, and we tried to stop him, because he was not following us." But Jesus said, "Do not stop him."
>
> —*Mark 9:38-39*

Prayer:

Generous God,

I struggle with the tension between conviction and tolerance. How easy it is to slip into an attitude of bigotry and sincerely believe I am standing for you when, in fact, my attitude toward others is anything but loving.

I know how strong the power of evil is in this world. It is not always like a roaring lion; rather, more often than not, evil is subtle and disguised. Wherever I look, I can see its destructive effects in people's lives.

Yet the Evil One blinds the eyes of my understanding and claims my own soul by pride, envy, anger, and revenge. These demons must be cast out of my own spirit when others point them out to me.

Forgive me when I fall into the subtle trap of nurturing these attitudes.

It seems as though I am always trying to determine who is in and who is out. People who are different from me scare me. If people understand and practice their faith in ways that are contrary to my traditions and beliefs, it is easy to place them outside the scope of your love. If they worship in ways that make no sense to me or interpret your Word differently from my point of view, it is easy to dismiss them and deny their claim to my love.

Forgive me when I fall into the subtle trap of creating
my own little family within the community of
your grace.
If I disagree with others, it is hard for me to see your goodness
in them.
I even find myself wanting them to fail and doing
everything possible to make sure they do not succeed.
But you often choose those people I would least expect
for your service. People who are powerless are often the
most effective witnesses to the power of your love.
Forgive me when I fall into the subtle trap of denying
that you can work through any of your children
in any situation.
Forgive me, Lord, for frequently being so fond of my group,
my opinion, my church, my religion. Forgive me too for
displaying bigotry in my actions toward others or hiding it
in attitudes no one can see. Enable me to discern your
presence in every kind and loving action. Give me the
wisdom to embrace truth wherever it may be found. And
never allow the intolerance and bigotry of others to be an
excuse for my own. Amen.

Hymn:

> Lord, that I may learn of thee,
> Give me true simplicity;
> Wean my soul, and keep it low,
> Willing thee alone to know.
>
> Let me cast my reeds aside,
> All that feeds my knowing pride,
> Not to man, but God submit,
> Lay my reasonings at thy feet.
>
> Then infuse the teaching grace,
> Spirit of truth and righteousness;
> Knowledge, love divine impart,
> Life eternal to my heart.

(Collection 293:1, 2, 4)

39 🐦
Catholic Spirit

Scripture:

> When he left there, he met Jehonadab son of Rechab
> coming to meet him; he greeted him, and said to him,
> "Is your heart as true to mine as mine is to yours?"
> Jehonadab answered, "It is." Jehu said, "If it is, give me
> your hand."
>
> *—2 Kings 10:15*

Prayer:

Welcoming God,

    In Jesus Christ you call us to love all of our brothers and
        sisters in one family.

        While not all of us can think alike or walk alike, surely we
           can all love alike. If we are of one heart, surely we can
           join our hands together!

    You are not really concerned about our peculiar opinions or
        how we worship.

        What matters is having a heart rooted in your love,
           believing in Jesus Christ as our Lord and Savior,
           being filled with all the energy of your love,
           doing your will and serving you in every way,
           loving our neighbors as we love ourselves,

and demonstrating that love through
  our concrete actions.
People all around us cry out,
  "Is there anyone who really loves me?"
  Empower us with a love that is long-suffering and kind
    and patient,
    a love that never envies and is never provoked,
    a love that only thinks the best of other people,
      covers all things, believes all things, and hopes all
        things.
Give us grace, O welcoming God, to encourage one another
  to pray,
  to inspire one another to be more loving
    in both words and deeds,
  and to challenge one another to love
    as Christ has loved us.
Fill us with a "catholic spirit"—a spirit that takes seriously
  what we believe about essential matters but does not make
  our own opinions the rule for all,
  a spirit that takes seriously the need to practice our faith
    but does not claim to possess all the truth.
  While we steadfastly practice our faith in Jesus Christ,
    believe the truth you have revealed to us in him,
      worship you in the ways that are most nourishing to
        our souls,
      and grow in our discipleship within our own loving
        family,
      enlarge our hearts to encompass all of your children.
  Empower us to run the race that is set before us,
    in the royal way of universal love. Amen.

Hymn:

> All praise to our redeeming Lord,
>   who joins us by his grace,
> and bids us, each to each restored,
>   together seek his face.
>
> He bids us build each other up;
>   and, gathered into one,
> to our high calling's glorious hope
>   we hand in hand go on.

(UMH 554:1, 2)

40 🖝
Christian Perfection

Scripture:

> Not that I have already obtained this or have already
> reached the goal.
>
> —*Philippians 3:12*

Prayer:

God of Perfect Love,

You call me to be perfect even as you are perfect. That is a
monumental claim upon my life. Despite the fact that this
call to be completely conformed to the image of Christ—
to be absolutely Christlike in my life—is offensive to
many, I will strive to open my life to the transforming
power of your perfecting love. My prayer is that I might
become daily more and more like Jesus, your Son.

The perfection to which you call me certainly does not mean
that I will ever be free from ignorance or mistakes or
infirmities or temptation; neither is it a call to absolute
perfection, for only your unconditional love is perfect in
this sense.

Rather you call me quite simply to develop such a close and
loving relationship with you that I would never want to do
anything to separate myself from that love or withhold it

from anyone else. You call me to be loving as Christ was loving, in every relationship and at all times. And if I live by your grace in this way, then I will always be able to look you in the face without fear and with love in my eyes.

So I pray sincerely that the blood of Christ might cleanse me from all sin. I know that you are ready to forgive all the darkness of my past and that you are able to fill my heart with your life-transforming Spirit. I know that Jesus is my advocate, a liberator who frees me from the bondage of my past and sets my course for a future filled with reconciling and liberating love.

I pray that you also free me from those thoughts and desires that are contrary to your love. I want to be clean, not only on the outside but also inside. If I am to be like Christ, his love must rule alone on the throne of my heart. I want you to live in me and become the source of all my thoughts, words, and actions.

Purify me from pride, from self-will, and from anger.

Grant me courage to press on toward the mark for the prize of your high calling in Jesus Christ, not because I can make it my own but because you have made me your own. Make me mature in him through the power of your Spirit, and perfect me in your love. Amen.

Hymn:

> To love is all my wish,
> I only live for this:
> Grant me, Lord, my heart's desire,
> There by faith for ever dwell.
> This I always will require,
> Thee, and only thee to feel.

Ah! give me this to know,
With all thy saints below;
Swells my soul to compass thee;
Gasps in thee to live and move;
Filled with all the Deity,
All immersed and lost in love!

(Collection 26:4, 6)

41 ✍

Wandering Thoughts

Scripture:

> We take every thought captive to obey Christ.
>
> —*2 Corinthians 10:5*

Prayer:

Patient Friend,

I am often plagued by wandering thoughts. While I make
every effort to keep my mind focused on you and to keep
my thoughts holy, just, and good, I all too frequently fail.
My thoughts often take up a life of their own.

I suppose I need to realize that you don't intend for me to be
conscious of your presence in every thought I think. That is
not realistic. What I need to be concerned about are
thoughts that are incompatible with your love and
presence, thoughts that woo me away from you.

Guard me, therefore, from the attitude of pride and anger and
revenge, for these thoughts certainly create a barrier
between us that I do not want to see built up.

When my thoughts wander because of sickness, lack of sleep,
pain or pleasure, interruptions or distractions, don't let me
take myself too seriously. Reassure me that you are always
there despite the fact that I am often not.

Stop me from feeding on ideas that can only have destructive
ends, and deliver me from the power of ever-present,
lurking evil.

Rather help me to fill my mind with what is noble and good
and true. Enable me to leave a wide space for you, a large
room for you, in my mind as well as my heart. If need be,
lull me to rest in your arms.

Above all, and regardless of where I find my mind wandering
on this occasion or that, may all the rambling of heart and
mind work together for good, as it will if left in your
guiding hand. Amen.

Hymn:

> Show me, as my soul can bear,
>   The depth of inbred sin,
> All the unbelief declare,
>   The pride that lurks within;
> Take me, whom thyself hast bought,
>   Bring into captivity
> Every high aspiring thought
>   That would not stoop to thee.
>
> Lord, my time is in thy hand,
>   My soul to thee convert;
> Thou canst make me understand,
>   Though I am slow of heart;
> Thine, in whom I live and move,
>   Thine the work, the praise is thine,
> Thou art wisdom, power, and love—
>   And all thou art is mine.

(Collection 348:4, 5)

42 ❧
Satan's Devices

Scripture:

> We are not ignorant of [Satan's] designs.
>
> —*2 Corinthians 2:11*

Prayer:

God, Our Fortress and Our Strength,

We expect to be made perfect in love in this life. We trust in your promise that a time will come when we shall do your will, live a life of purity, and in all our words and deeds give thanks to you. But the grand design of Satan is to destroy all of your work in our soul.

Satan desires to dampen our joy in your love by reminding us continually of our brokenness and failings, by attacking our peace, by attempting to persuade us that the darkness in our life is more powerful than the light, and by assaulting the holiness we have received from you.

Most importantly, Satan wants to shake our desire to be as Christlike as we can possibly be by putting doubts and fears in our mind. He wants to weaken and destroy our faith, for this is the only foundation of a loving and holy life. By destroying our vision of your goal for us all, he believes he can trip us up in the race.

So subtle are the ways of the Adversary that he attempts to

divide the gospel against itself. He destroys the foundation of the Christian life by fixing our mind on the goal apart from the means of getting there—by making us think we can be loving without faith. Or he persuades us of the impossibility of becoming loving people in this life—by focusing all of our attention on what we will receive from you hereafter, making us neglect what we have already received.

There is no more potent barrier to our quest for holiness than impatience and envy concerning your great promise to us. How easy it is to become more unholy than we were by pursuing the grand goal of perfect love with a perverted motivation or an unloving attitude.

But you provide the necessary means to guide us down the right path.

When we lose our joy in life because of brokenness and pain, we will rejoice in the hope of healing.

When we lose our sense of peace because of the long way toward the goal of perfect love, we will put our trust in the gift of Christ.

When we are tempted to abandon our faith altogether, we will place our confidence in your immeasurable love all the more.

We rejoice in the lives of your loving people who surround us. Draw us, with them, in our pilgrimage with Christ into the center of your love. Amen.

Hymn:

> Eternal, spotless Lamb of God,
> Before the world's foundation slain,
> Sprinkle us ever with thy blood;
> O cleanse, and keep us ever clean!
> To every soul (all praise to thee)
> Our [feelings] of compassion move,
> And all mankind by this may see
> God is in us—for God is love.
>
> Giver and Lord of life, whose power
> And guardian care for all are free,
> To thee, in fierce temptation's hour,
> From sin and Satan let us flee;
> Thine, Lord, we are, and ours thou art;
> In us be all thy goodness showed,
> Renew, enlarge, and fill our heart
> With peace, and joy, and heaven, and God.

(Collection 227:1, 2)

43 ✍

The Scripture Way of Salvation

Scripture:

> For by grace you have been saved through faith.

—*Ephesians 2:8*

Prayer:

God of Restoration,

Thank you for offering me salvation here and now as a
blessing possessed in the present moment and not simply
hoped for in a distant future.

Thank you for reaching out to me with your love
before I even knew your name.

Thank you for enveloping me in that love and wooing me
into your embrace.

Thank you for making me safe through your gift of faith in
Jesus Christ.

Thank you for pardoning my sins and accepting me without
reservation as your child.

Thank you for taking the initiative to bridge the gap that
separates us from you—a change in relationship that leads
me to rejoice in hope.

Thank you for giving me a second birth, a new beginning—
a real change that makes it possible for me to be more and

more dead to sin and more and more
alive in your love.
Thank you for the promise of perfect love in my life, a love
that excludes all sin and fills my heart with a capacity to
love you and all others
that I never dreamed possible.
You have opened my eyes and illuminated my soul
by your Spirit.
And the Spirit has gifted me with the conviction that
Christ loved *me*
and gave himself for *me.*
With this assurance comes the confidence, trust, and reliance
that I need to remain steadfast in your love.
In all of this, O Lord—in both my acceptance of your
embrace and your restoration of my life—faith, or simple
trust in you, is the key.
A childlike trust in your love is the only thing I need to
find my way back home and take my place in
your family of love.
All I desire then is to grow in your grace as I practice
the works of piety and mercy that reflect the spirit
of Christ.
Above all things, you are a God of promise and a God of love.
Fulfill your dream for my life for the sake of Jesus Christ.
Purify my heart and fill it with all the fullness of your love.
I believe that you are willing and able to fill my heart to
overflowing at any moment by your grace.
Lord, I want to be like Jesus, now. Amen.

Hymn:

> O for a thousand tongues to sing
> My dear Redeemer's praise!
> The glories of my God and King,
> The triumphs of his grace!
>
> My gracious Master, and my God,
> Assist me to proclaim,
> To spread through all the earth abroad
> The honours of thy name.
>
> Look unto him, ye nations, own
> Your God, ye fallen race;
> Look, and be saved through faith alone,
> Be justified by grace!

(Collection 1:1, 2, 6)

44 ✒
Original Sin

Scripture:

> The Lord saw that the wickedness of humankind was great in the earth, and that every inclination of the thoughts of their hearts was only evil continually.
>
> —*Genesis 6:5*

Prayer:

Great Physician of my soul,

    When I consider how terribly people behave toward one another and reflect on the brokenness of life, I want to weep.

    Despite the fact that you created me in your own image and called me good, I once lived my life as if I never knew you; my heart and mind were ruled by prideful concern for self and so seldom reflected the purity, justice, mercy, and truth that you intend. I wanted to be god.

        The psalmist David proclaims that everyone is lost in this way.

        The prophet Isaiah declares that the whole head is sick and the whole heart, faint.

    But you opened my eyes and showed me that I was living without you.

You demonstrated that you not only wanted me to
acknowledge you as God but that you actually yearned
for me to love you.
Despite the fact that pride controlled my life from
beginning to end,
despite the fact that my own will was more important
to me than anything else except the desire for praise,
despite the fact that I tried to find happiness in
everything you had created rather than in your
amazing love for me,
you never abandoned me and loved me still.
The first step toward my healing was to acknowledge how far
I was from you and how deliberately I had turned my back
on your love and your ways. In Christ you began to heal
my soul, you began the divine therapy that would bring
me back to wholeness and peace. You showed me that
Christ loved *me* and gave himself for *me*. And when I had
truly come to myself—when I finally realized I was your
child—you began to heal the self-inflicted wounds and
pains in my life.
Great Physician, if I had never fallen, there would have been
no need for your amazing work of love in my heart, this
renewal of my spirit. But you have helped me to know my
disease. You have shown me my cure. You have given me
a new birth and a fresh start through my faith in Jesus
Christ. By your grace I shall be fully restored and find my
way home. Amen.

Hymn:

O Jesus, full of truth and grace,
   More full of grace than I of sin,
Yet once again I seek thy face;
   Open thine arms and take me in,
And freely my backslidings heal,
And love the faithless sinner still.

The stone of flesh again convert!
   The veil of sin again remove!
Drop thy warm blood upon my heart,
   And melt it by thy dying love!
This rebel heart by love subdue,
And make it soft, and make it new.

(Collection 179:2, 4)

45 🔊
New Birth

Scripture:

> You must be born from above.

—John 3:7

Prayer:

Re-Creating God,

You have done such a marvelous thing for us in forgiving our
sins in Christ.

You have worked such a miraculous change in us by renewing
our broken lives through the power of your Spirit.

Both the forgiveness and the renewal are essential to our
becoming whole.

We are physically born to new life in this world. You reshape
our spirits through a new birth from above made possible
through Christ.

You created us in your own image. Because you are love, you
created us to be full of love. Because you are full of justice,
mercy, and truth, you created us to be holy in every way.
Because you are pure, you created us to live in harmony,
caring for and loving one another.

In a willful act of disobedience we rebelled against you, O
God, lost both your image and your life, and experienced

the awful pain of spiritual death. That is why we must be born again—to rediscover life.

How you are able to birth us anew will always be a great mystery. Our spiritual rebirth is similar in so many ways to our first birth. Before we were born into this world, we had eyes but could not see.

In the same way, before you birth us anew in Christ, our spiritual senses are locked up—dead. When we experience the power of your unconditional love, it is like being born again, it is like breathing for the very first time, it is like being created anew to be like Jesus in every way and as you have always intended us to be.

Through the sacrament of baptism you have given us an outward and visible sign of this inward and spiritual change in our lives. It is a potent symbol, but it is not the change itself. We need both the sign and what it symbolizes. We need the sign-act of your love in baptism, which proclaims your love for each of us unconditionally. And we need for you to re-create us in the image of Christ—your image of love.

You re-create us in Christ, O God, to be holy, to be loving and generous, merciful, kind, and just in all our relationships in life.

You re-create us in Christ, O God, so that we might be able to look you squarely in the face, to live with you and enjoy you forever.

You re-create us in Christ, O God, simply because you want all of your children to be truly happy now. Amen.

Hymn:

> O come, and dwell in me,
> Spirit of power within,
> And bring the glorious liberty
> From sorrow, fear, and sin.
> The seed of sin's disease,
> Spirit of health, remove,
> Spirit of finished holiness,
> Spirit of perfect love.
>
> Hasten the joyful day
> Which shall my sins consume,
> When old things shall be passed away,
> And all things new become.
> Th'original offence
> Out of my soul erase;
> Enter thyself, and drive it hence,
> And take up all the place.

(Collection 356:1, 2)

46 ❧
The Wilderness State

So you have pain now; but I will see you again, and
your hearts will rejoice, and no one will take your joy
from you.

—*John 16:22*

Prayer:

Guiding and Comforting God,
   Sometimes I feel as though I am in the midst of a vast and
      lonely wilderness.
      The strong faith and sense of your love that I had seems to
         disappear.
      I cannot love others as I know I should. I have no sense of
         joy or peace in my life, and I am an easy prey to
         temptation.
   You have no desire for me to feel abandoned. In Christ you
      know the depth of that pain and the anguish it creates.
      I know that you will never desert me! And yet I feel so
      all alone!
   When I look deep inside myself, and especially when I reflect
      on my relationship with you, it is clear that darkness creeps
      into my life whenever I turn my back on you. Sometimes I

turn my back by doing things I know are wrong; more
frequently, I turn my back by not acting in a loving way.

Forgive me for my neglect of private prayer,

for giving way to inward sin—pride, anger, and unhealthy
desires that erode my love of you,

for succumbing to outward sin—words and deeds that
hurt others, destroy relationships, and breed
disharmony.

When I look deep inside myself, I also see how ignorant I am
of your ways. When I cannot quickly discern your activity
in my life, I feel alone, despite the fact that you are always
present and loving me still.

When I look deep inside myself, I realize how easily I am led
astray from your path. When I fail to rely on you in the
face of these temptations, thinking I can handle them
myself, then I put out your light, and all turns to darkness
around me.

Whenever I feel lost or abandoned, help me to find my way
home by searching my heart and finding you there, ready
to welcome, to forgive, and to embrace.

If my sin stands in the way of a deeper fellowship with
you, then change my heart through the healing
presence of the Spirit.

If ignorance leaves me in the darkness, then draw me into
the light through the power of your love.

If temptation clouds my clear vision of you, then deliver
me from evil so that you reign in my life.

Whenever I feel abandoned and alone, enable me to learn
and to grow through the pain, to cling to you even as you
support me in the struggle, and, ultimately, to find my way
home. Amen.

Hymn:

> Jesus, the gift divine I know,
>   The gift divine I ask of thee;
> That living water now bestow,
>   Thy Spirit and thyself on me.
> Thou, Lord, of life the fountain art:
> Now let me find thee in my heart!
>
> Thee let me drink, and thirst no more
>   For drops of finite happiness;
> Spring up, O well, in heavenly power,
>   In streams of pure, perennial peace,
> In peace, that none can take away,
> In joy, which shall forever stay.

(Collection 354:1, 2)

47 ❧
A Heavy Heart

Scripture:

> In this you rejoice, even if now for a little while you have
> had to suffer various trials.
>
> —*1 Peter 1.6*

Prayer:

O Guardian of my soul,

My heart is heavy. My faith is still strong, peace keeps my
heart and mind in Christ Jesus my Lord, and I am filled
with a living hope. The Holy Spirit is the great joy of my
life, and I still love you above all things, striving to be holy
in both heart and life. But my heart is heavy.

I am heavy with grief and with sorrow. This heaviness is so
deep that it seems to overshadow my whole soul and every
aspect of my life.

It seems as though all of my energy is being drained from
me in order to deal with this great trial that I feel inside.

I am being attacked by all kinds of temptations from all
directions.

My body is out of control, racked with pain and disease
and disorder.

I am hungry and poor, and death seems to be at the door.

Even worse, I grieve for those I love who live as though
they were dead. Why can they not experience your love?
The question plagues me day and night,
Have you left me alone?
Is my brokenness so great, my fallenness so grave, that I
will never know what true love is?
My heart is heavy, O Guardian of my soul.
Refine my faith; purify, confirm, and increase within me a
living hope and joy in the Lord that I might love you
with an undying love.
In the midst of my despair, birth faith and hope and love
in order for me to find healing in my praise of you and
your compassion.
My heart is heavy, but in you, O God, I place my complete
trust, for you guard my soul as a parent loves a child. In
you there is light, and the darkness will never put out the
light of your love. Amen.

Hymn:

Human tears may freely flow
Authorised by tears Divine,
Till Thine awful will we know,
Comprehend Thy whole design:
Jesus wept! and so may we:
Jesus, suffering all Thy will,
Felt the soft infirmity;
Feels His Creature's sorrow still.

Jesus blends them with His own,
Mindful of His suffering days:
Father, hear Thy pleading Son,

Son of Man for us He prays:
What for us He asks, bestow:
Ours He makes His own request:
Send us life or death; we know,
Life, or death from Thee is best.

(Tyson 126:4, 7)

48 ⟡
Self-Denial

Scripture:

> Then he said to them all, "If any want to become my followers, let them deny themselves and take up their cross daily and follow me."
>
> —*Luke 9:23*

Prayer:

Purifying God,

You command me to deny myself, to take up my cross and follow wherever you lead. I cannot become or continue as your disciple unless I respond to your call with absolute seriousness. And it is no easy thing.

On one hand, your command is difficult for me because everyone in my world today cringes at the thought of self-denial. On the other hand, even some Christians claim that taking such a demand seriously is the trap of legalism—succumbing to the temptation of salvation by works.

And yet, your word to us and the witness of Jesus Christ is very clear.

For me to deny myself means to follow not my own will but yours.

How easy this would be if our two wills were the same, but more often than not, I find my selfish desires at odds with your way. Your love is broad and mine is very narrow.

To take up the cross means I must pick up whatever lies in my path to your love.

How nice it would be if this simply led to ease and joy.

But to take up my cross is essentially painful, and a part of taking it up is bearing its weight.

To bear my cross is to endure what is laid upon me without my choice.

To take up my cross is to suffer voluntarily what I have the power to avoid.

To pick up and carry the cross designed for me means to embrace your will, O God, even though it is not what I want.

Taking up and bearing the cross defines my life as a disciple of Christ.

This is what makes me different from all your children who remain outside the household of faith though never beyond the reach of your love.

My unwillingness to deny self is always the greatest barrier to your love. Your love is freely given but never embraced by the one who trusts only in self:

he who is dead in sin does not awake,

she who begins to awake has no lasting conviction,

he who is convinced he is lost never experiences the liberating pardon from sin,

she who has attained your great gift does not return it.

None of these gets beyond himself or herself.

Form me into a true disciple of Jesus Christ, O purifying God, and conform every aspect of my life to the shape of the cross. May I know in the very core of my being that I will never find the real meaning of life until I have the courage to give it away. Then, having died with Christ, raise me into a new life of never-ending love and light. Amen.

Hymn:

> O God, what offering shall I give
>   To thee, the Lord of earth and skies?
> My spirit, soul, and flesh receive,
>   A holy, living sacrifice!
> Small as it is, 'tis all my store—
> More shouldst thou have, if I had more.
>
> Thou hast my flesh, thy hallowed shrine,
>   Devoted solely to thy will;
> Here let thy light for ever shine;
>   This house still let thy presence fill;
> O source of life, live, dwell, and move
> In me, till all my life be love.

(Collection 419:1, 3)

49 ❧
Reconciliation in the Church

Scripture:

> If another member of the church sins against you, go and
> point out the fault when the two of you are alone. If the
> member listens to you, you have regained that one. But if
> you are not listened to, take one or two others along with
> you, so that every word may be confirmed by the evi-
> dence of two or three witnesses. If the member refuses to
> listen to them, tell it to the church; and if the offender
> refuses to listen even to the church, let such a one be to
> you as a Gentile and a tax collector.
>
> —*Matthew 18:15-17*

Prayer:

God of Reconciliation,

You have called us to be ambassadors of healing and
  understanding in Christ. Yet it is easy for us to make
  ourselves feel good by pointing out failures in others. We
  talk about others behind their back. We are so frequently
  unfair. Forgive us, we pray. Plant a spirit of reconciliation
  within us.

When others within our community of faith make mistakes
  or turn their back on you, rather than approaching them

with a spirit of tender love, gentleness, and meekness, we
nurture pride and contempt in our heart. Rather than
dealing with our brothers and sisters directly and with
genuine concern, we gossip and judge.
Forgive us, we pray.
Plant a spirit of reconciliation within us.
Lord, we need to help one another in our journey of faith,
and all of us make many mistakes and get lost along the
way. All of us need to learn gentleness, patience, and
kindness from one another. Love ought to determine how
we deal with our brothers and sisters in your family.
Everyone needs to be understood, and often we need the
counsel of others who see what we are doing better than
we see for ourselves. We need to be accountable to one
another because that is the only way we can continue to
grow in your love.
Forgive us, we pray.
Plant a spirit of reconciliation within us.
We are a part of your community, the church. The whole
point of our common life together is learning how to love
and then sharing that love with everyone you bring into
our path. Whenever we hurt one another by our words or
our actions, move us toward reconciliation quickly. Help
us to be honest with one another but always to speak the
truth in love. We want to be your faithful family of healing
and of love.
Forgive us, we pray.
Plant a spirit of reconciliation within us.
Heal our broken relationships and make us one in Christ our
Lord. Amen.

Hymn:

> Christ, from whom all blessings flow,
> Perfecting the saints below,
> Hear us, who thy nature share,
> Who thy mystic body are.
>
> Join us, in one spirit join,
> Let us still receive of thine;
> Still for more on thee we call,
> Thee who fillest all in all!
>
> Sweetly may we all agree,
> Touched with softest sympathy;
> Kindly for each other care,
> Every member feel its share.

(Collection 504:1, 2, 7)

50 ✒

The Use of Money

Scripture:

> And I tell you, make friends for yourselves by means of dishonest wealth so that when it is gone, they may welcome you into the eternal homes.
>
> —*Luke 16:9*

Prayer:

Steward of All Life,

Three rules are essential to the proper use of my resources.

Enable me to *gain* all I can.

But as you bless my labors, guard me from harming my
health, my mind, or my neighbor in the process.

May honest work and common sense be my guide.

Encourage me to *save* all I can.

Guard me from wasting your precious resources to gratify
unhealthy and prideful desires.

May the most important legacy I leave behind be that of
justice, integrity, and generosity.

And so empower me to *give* all I can.

In my efforts to be a good steward of your many blessings,
give me what I need to provide caringly for those I love,
open my heart to the needs of those who are close
at hand,

and create a generous spirit within me to do good to all.
You have blessed my life in so many ways. As I seek to be a
faithful steward of all I have received from your hand, may
I keep these questions foremost in my mind:
Am I acting according to my character as a steward?
Am I obedient to your Word and your calling upon
my life?
Can I offer up this act of kindness or generosity as a
sacrifice to you though Jesus Christ?
Is my spirit loving and consistent with your eternal
concerns?
Teach me, O generous God, what it means to be a steward of
your treasures. Amen.

Hymn:

The poor, as Jesus' bosom-friends,
The poor he makes his latest care,
To all his successors commends,
And wills us on our hands to bear:
The poor our dearest care we make,
Aspiring to superior bliss,
And cherish for their Saviour's sake,
And love them with a love like his.

(Kimbrough II, 404)

51 🐦
The Good Steward

Scripture:

> Give me an accounting of your management, because
> you cannot be my manager any longer.
>
> —*Luke 16:2*

Prayer:

Blessed and Giving God,

Since nothing in this life is properly my own, I am not at
liberty to use your blessings as I please.

You have entrusted me with my soul, my body, my goods,
and my talents.

You call me to watch over my soul, made in your image, to
guard my understanding, imagination, memory, will,
and affections.

You describe my body as the temple of your Holy Spirit.

You bless my life with food and clothing, shelter and money.

To all of this you add strength and health, knowledge and
learning, influence and time—grace upon grace.

You are a generous God who has blessed me in every
imaginable way.

My stewardship over these riches is a momentary thing. But
while some of your blessings are here today and gone

tomorrow, others are eternal and forever bear the imprint
of my care or my neglect.
And so it is important for to ask:
  Do I properly care for my soul?
  Do I use my body to your glory?
  Do I share my worldly possessions in just and loving
    ways?
  Do I exercise a faithful stewardship of my talents?
When I stop in the course of my busy life to reflect on your
  blessedness, I see how precious are all your gifts!
Help me to use every means possible, therefore, to grow
  in grace.
Remind me continually that since everything I have or am
  is a gracious blessing from you, everything I can do for
  you is simply a mark of my gratitude for your love.
Above all help me to remember that despite all my
  resolutions, my patience, and my constancy, in the end,
  it is your grace that is sufficient! Amen.

Hymn:

A charge to keep I have,
A God to glorify,
A never-dying soul to save,
And fit it for the sky;
To serve the present age,
My calling to fulfill;
O may it all my powers engage
To do my Master's will!

Arm me with jealous care,
  As in thy sight to live;
And Oh! thy servant, Lord, prepare
  A strict account to give.

(Collection 309:1, 2)

52 🙠
Agents of Shalom

Scripture:

> Who rises up for me against the wicked?
>
> —*Psalm 94:16*

Prayer:

Just and Loving God,

You call us to offer your love to all of your children, to oppose
injustice wherever we find it, and to promote your reign of
shalom on earth.

For the many times we have failed to be an obedient
church, we ask you to forgive us.

Strengthen our resolve to confess Christ by being your
agents of justice, peace, and love in an unjust and
ungodly world.

Grant us courage, steadfast God of justice and love,

to honor your name by waging peace,

to reflect your compassion by empowering people
to change their lives by your grace,

to obey your law of love by offering Christ to all.

If we are to be the agents of your transforming love,

we must not only fear you but love you;

we must not only be harmless but be people of faith,
  courage, and patience;
we must not only express concern for our neighbors but
  love them as brothers and sisters in the world, our
  earthly home.
Enable humility to flow from our hearts, which are filled with
  your love,
  and compassion to pour from the Spirit of Christ, which
  dwells within.
Keep our motives focused on your glory and the good of all.
Join innocence with prudence, seriousness with a tender and
  loving spirit.
And when the cross seems too heavy, the work too hard, the
  insults too sharp, the barriers too high, and the dangers
  too great—
  when we are ready to give up all hope—
  help us to commit our souls, our bodies, and all that we
  have and are to Christ.
For nothing is more important than our remaining faithful
  to him and to his winsome way of love. Amen.

Hymn:

Rejoice, the Lord is King!
  Your Lord and King adore;
mortals, give thanks and sing,
  and triumph evermore.
Lift up your heart, lift up your voice;
rejoice; again I say, rejoice.

His kingdom cannot fail;
  he rules o'er earth and heaven;

the keys of earth and hell
     are to our Jesus given.
Lift up your heart, lift up your voice;
rejoice; again I say, rejoice.

(UMH 715:1, 3)

Wesley's Original Sermon Titles
〜

The original titles under which Wesley's sermons were published appear below with the titles used in this volume in italics.

1. Salvation by Faith (*Salvation by Faith*)
2. The Almost Christian (*Altogether Christian*)
3. Awake, Thou That Sleepest (*Spiritual Awakenings*)
4. Scriptural Christianity (*Scriptural Christianity*)
5. Justification by Faith (*Justification by Faith*)
6. The Righteousness of Faith (*The Righteousness of Faith*)
7. The Way to the Kingdom (*The Way to Shalom*)
8. The First Fruits of the Spirit (*No Condemnation*)
9. The Spirit of Bondage and Adoption (*From Fear to Love*)
10. The Witness of the Spirit (*The Witness of the Spirit*)
11. The Witness of the Spirit, 2 (*Assurance and Its Fruit*)
12. The Witness of Our Own Spirit (*Christian Conscience*)
13. On Sin in Believers (*Remaining Sin*)
14. The Repentance of Believers (*Continuing Repentance*)
15. The Great Assize (*The Great Judgment*)
16. The Means of Grace (*Means of Grace*)
17. The Circumcision of the Heart (*A Heart for God*)
18. The Marks of the New Birth (*Marks of New Birth*)
19. The Great Privilege of Those That Are Born of God (*Christian Privileges*)
20. The Lord Our Righteousness (*The Righteousness of Christ*)
21. Upon Our Lord's Sermon on the Mount, I (*Yearning for God*)

Scripture Index of Sermon Texts
❧

THE OLD TESTAMENT (Hebrew Scriptures)

Scripture Text	Sermon Number
Genesis 6:5	44
2 Kings 10:15	39
Psalm 94:16	52
Jeremiah 23:6	20
Malachi 3:7	16

THE NEW TESTAMENT

Scripture Text	Sermon Number
Matthew 5:1-4	21
Matthew 5:5-7	22
Matthew 5:8-12	23
Matthew 5:13-16	24
Matthew 5:17-20	25
Matthew 6:1-15	26
Matthew 6:16-18	27
Matthew 6:19-23	28
Matthew 6:24-34	29
Matthew 7:1-12	30
Matthew 7:13-14	31
Matthew 7:15-20	32
Matthew 7:21-27	33

Scripture Text	Sermon Number
Matthew 18:15-17	49
Mark 1:15	7 and 14
Mark 9:38-39	38
Luke 9:23	48
Luke 16:2	51
Luke 16:9	50
John 3:7	45
John 3:8	18
John 16:22	46
Acts 4:31	4
Acts 26:24	37
Acts 26:28	2
Romans 2:29	17
Romans 3:31	35 and 36
Romans 4:5	5
Romans 7:12	4
Romans 8:1-4	8
Romans 8:15	9
Romans 8:16	10 and 11
Romans 10:5-8	6
Romans 14:10	15
2 Corinthians 1:12	12
2 Corinthians 2:11	42
2 Corinthians 5:17	13
2 Corinthians 10:5	41
Ephesians 2:8	1 and 43
Ephesians 5:14	3
Philippians 3:12	40
1 Peter 1:6	47
1 John 3:9	19

Index of Hymns
꙳

In the following index the hymn selections are placed in numerical sequence as they appear in the 1780 *A Collection of Hymns for the Use of the People Called Methodists*. The numbers following the colon indicate the stanzas of the hymn. Selections from the other hymn sources are noted at the conclusion of the index.

Hymn Sources

Collection: Hildebrandt, Franz and Beckerlegge, Oliver A., eds. *The Works of John Wesley. Volume 7. A Collection of Hymns for the Use of the People Called Methodists*. Nashville, Tenn.: Abingdon Press, 1983.

Kimbrough: Kimbrough, S T, Jr. and Beckerlegge, Oliver A., eds. *The Unpublished Poetry of Charles Wesley. Volume 2. Hymns and Poems on Holy Scripture*. Nashville, Tenn.: Kingswood Books, 1990.

HLS: Rattenbury, J. Ernest. *The Eucharistic Hymns of John and Charles Wesley*. London: The Epworth Press, 1948.

Tyson: Tyson, John R., ed. *Charles Wesley: A Reader*. Oxford: Oxford University Press, 1989.

UMH: *The United Methodist Hymnal*. Nashville, Tenn.: The United Methodist Publishing House, 1989.

Hymn	First Line	Sermon
1: 1, 2, 6	O for a thousand tongues to sing	43
16: 1, 3	Happy the souls that first believed	4
26: 4, 6	Saviour, the world's and mine	40
53: 1, 5	Hearken to the solemn voice	15
65: 1, 2	How weak the thoughts and vain	33
69: 1, 6	Leader of faithful souls, and guide	31
81: 5, 7	Thou Son of God, whose flaming eyes	3
86: 1, 2, 3	Father of all, in whom alone	34
93: 4, 5	How can a sinner know	10
102: 1, 2	O that I could repent	7
103: 2, 8	Jesu, let thy pitying eye	14
106: 5, 6	Jesu, Friend of sinners, hear	19
130: 1, 2	Jesu, if still the same thou art	21
130: 3, 6	Jesu, if still the same thou art	22
139: 3, 5	O Jesus, let me bless thy name	20
179: 2, 4	Weary of wand'ring from my God	44
183: 1, 8	Jesu, thy blood and righteousness	5
185: 1, 3	Oft I in my heart have said	6
193: 4, 5	And can it be, that I should gain	8
207: 1, 2, 3	Infinite, unexhausted Love	1
223: 1, 2	Happy man whom God doth aid	29
225: 1	Father of all, whose powerful voice	26
227: 1, 2	Eternal, spotless Lamb of God	42
227: 3	Eternal, spotless Lamb of God	26
293: 1, 2, 4	Lord, that I may learn of thee	38
299: 1, 2, 3	I want a principle within	12
301: 1, 5, 6	Into a world of ruffians sent	32
309: 1, 2	A charge to keep I have	51
323: 1, 5	Master, I own thy lawful claim	2
331: 2, 3	The thing my God doth hate	25

About the Author
✒

PAUL W. CHILCOTE is Professor of Church History and Wesleyan Studies at Asbury Theological Seminary in Orlando, Florida. He was a charter member of the Africa University School of Theology in Mutare, Zimbabwe, serving there from 1992–94 as Senior Lecturer in Church History. With his wife, Janet, he served as Missionary-in-Residence at the Methodist Theological School in Ohio, and he was a Lecturer at St. Paul's United Theological College in Limuru, Kenya. Dr. Chilcote frequently leads workshops on Wesleyan studies, Christian spirituality, and discipleship.

Recommended Reading
✎

We hope you have enjoyed this book and are interested in reading other resources published by The Upper Room. Here are a few of our recommendations.

Wesleyan resources:
A Longing for Holiness: Selected Writings of John Wesley #827
Devotional Life in the Wesleyan Tradition by Steve Harper #467
Devotional Life in the Wesleyan Tradition: A Workbook by Steve Harper #740
As If the Heart Mattered: A Wesleyan Spirituality by Gregory S. Clapper #820

Other Prayer and Christian Formation Resources:
2000 Years Since Bethlehem: Images of Christ through the Centuries compiled by Janice T. Grana #865
A Book of Personal Prayer compiled by Rene Bideaux #812
Then Shall Your Light Rise: Spiritual Formation and Social Witness by Joyce Hollyday #816
Prayers for My Village by Michel Bouttier #711
Remember Who You Are: Baptism, A Model for Christian Life by William H. Willimon #399
Sunday Dinner: The Lord's Supper and the Christian Life by William H. Willimon #429
A Guide to Prayer for Ministers and Other Servants by Norman Shawchuck and Rueben P. Job #559 Paperback; #460 Gift edition
A Guide to Prayer for All God's People by Norman Shawchuck and Rueben P. Job #710 Paperback; #613 Gift edition
Upper Room Spiritual Classics:
  Series I: booklets featuring the writings of John Wesley, Teresa of Avila, Thomas Kelly, Augustine, and John Cassian #832
  Series II: booklets featuring the writings of Julian of Norwich,

Francis and Clare, Thomas à Kempis, Evelyn Underhill, and Toyohiko Kagawa #853
Series III: featuring writings from John of the Cross, The Desert Mothers and Fathers, William Law, John Woolman, and Catherine of Siena #905

Upper Room® books are available at most Christian bookstores or online at www.upperroom.org.

You may also order directly from The Upper Room® at 1-800-972-0433.